For Kid's Sake
Teaching Tackle Football
The Youth Coach's Field Manual
By: Ray Lieber

Library of Congress Catalog Card Number: 97-222052
ISBN 0-9659985-0-9

1997 Printing

Published by:
Youth Sports Press, Inc.
Pontchatrain Square
3433 Hwy. 190 #285
Mandeville, Louisiana 70471

Graphics and Illustration by Matt Gouig
Layout and Design by Jacquelyn Innerarity

Printed by
Mele Printing Company
100 Tyler Square
Covington, Louisiana 70433

Acknowledgment

The legendary Bear Bryant was once quoted as saying "One man doesn't make a team. It takes 11." Writing this manual demonstrated how critical teamwork is to any effort. It took a <u>team</u> of qualified and committed friends to make it happen. Their support and contributions have made this dream become a reality, and I will always be grateful to them.

Thanks to Mr. Matt Gouig, my illustrator, close friend and family member. He did a magnificent job with the artwork throughout the manual, including the logo for my model, and the cover design. He also deserves credit for the unique design of the icons, which are used to help guide the reader through the manual. Matt is more than just an illustrator, he is a creator; he brought my thoughts and images to life.

Thanks to Ms. Jackie Innerarity. Trust me when I say you can't play the game without a quarterback! Jackie is the best, and she has filled that role, plus many others during this project. She has supported me, both as managing and developmental editor. She is a gifted expert in the field of creative design and layout. She's guided me along the way, teaching and advising me, but more important, watching out for what's best for me. She has a level of dedication and commitment, which exceeds anyone's expectations. I can't imagine what I would have done without her help!

Thanks to Mr. Cliff St. Germain, Ph.D., and academic counselor. Cliff is an expert in the field of teaching and learning. He graciously volunteered his ideas and guidance to help me shape and communicate my ideas about teaching the youth athlete. Cliff and I share a common bond, and that is to help make a difference in the development of kids. He's a very creative and talented individual, and I'm truly indebted to him for his guidance.

Thanks to Mr. Roderick West, for his endorsement and support of this effort. For all of us who dream of our child's becoming the "Student/Athlete," Rod represents those standards. Throughout his education, he believed in excelling in the classroom first, and on the athletic field second. As a successful sports attorney, agent, and former standout on the 1988 Notre Dame National Championship Team under Lou Holtz, Rod knows the importance of developing sound values and beliefs in the young athlete. He is committed to helping kids understand that concept, and learning to take advantage of opportunity. I'm particularly grateful for the time he spent sharing his values and beliefs with my son.

Thanks to Mr. John Thompson, Assistant Head Coach/Defensive Coordinator at the University of Southern Mississippi. John is one of those professionals who dedicates his life to helping athletes achieve their dreams. He also understands and supports the role of the volunteer, who can make a difference in preparing kids to advance to the next level. I offer my sincerest thanks to him, for taking time out of his busy schedule to review and endorse the concepts and techniques provided in this manual. It's a lucky parent, and athlete, who get the opportunity to learn from him.

Thanks to my wife, Marlene and my son Aaron. I've learned you don't undertake a project of this effort without having to sacrifice something. Without their love and support, I could not have done this!

Acknowledgment continued

Finally, thanks to a special bunch of kids, who gave their time during the off-season to help me with this manual. Below is a photo of the young men displayed in the technique sections of this manual. Watching them play makes it all worthwhile!

Cheerleader Michele Bostwick. Kneeling First Row Left to Right: Carson Lockfield, Christopher Sistrunk, Kirk Bodenheimer, Josh Aymond. Standing Second Row Left to Right: Randy Rouyer, Kyle Nugent, Joel Ronzello, Conner Lockfield, Donnie Loehr. Not shown Eddie O'Connor.

Foreword

"Ray Lieber loves youth football! This book can help anyone who is interested in helping our young people enjoy the game of football.

Ray's tremendous knowledge and organizational skills, plus his insight, will be a guide to all who are involved with football at any level.

What Ray has discovered in his own life is available to you."

John Thompson
Assistant Head Coach / Defensive Coordinator
University of Southern Mississippi

"Ray Lieber incorporates a sound developmental philosophy and proven coaching techniques in what will likely to be one of the most influential contributions to little league football in a long time. It's easy to forget that the skills many of us took for granted as collegiate and professional athletes were actually taught at the little league level. For the veteran coaches and ex-players, Ray's manual provides an excellent teaching tool to help you convey your knowledge and expertise in the game to the young, hungry minds of the children you coach. For the first time football coach, this book will provide everything you need to succeed in what is a noble endeavor. This manual has it all. Great job Ray Lieber!"

Rod West
President
Notre Dame National Alumni Association

Table of Contents

INTRODUCTION   About This Manual

CHAPTER 1   The F.A.S.T Approach To Teaching Youth Football

CHAPTER 2   For Parent's Sake!

Table of Contents

Table of Contents

Table of Contents

Table of Contents

PLAYBOOK

Your Personal Offensive Strategy Planner:

Plays

T - Series	**Pro I and Slot I Series**
T 30 Blast vs. 6 - 2 Tight Defense	Pro-I 26 Power vs. 5 - 2 Okie Defense
T 44 Quick vs. 5 - 2 Okie Defense	Slot-I 31 Blast vs. 6 - 2 Tight Defense
T 26 Power vs. 6 - 2 Tight Defense	Pro-I 28 Toss Sweep vs. 6 - 2 Tight Defense
T 28 Sweep vs. Okie Defense	Slot-I 43 Counter vs. Okie Defense
T 43 Trap vs. 6 - 2 Tight	Pro-I 436 Drag vs. 6 - 2 Tight Defense
T 45 Rollout Pass	Pro-I 866 Slant vs. 6 - 2 Tight Defense
T 54 Bootleg Pass	
Wing - T Series	**Power I Series**
Wing-T 24 Trap	Power-I 25 Cutback vs. 6 - 2 Tight Defense
Wing-T 45 Buck Sweep	Power-I 18 Sweep vs. 5 - 2 Oklahoma Defense
Wing-T 44 Counter Trap	Power-I 26 Cross Buck
Wing-T 34 Wham vs. 6 - 2 Tight Defense	Power-I 46 Drop Back 5 - 2 Okie Defense
Wing-T 345 Throwback vs. 5 - 2 Oklahoma Defense	

Appendix

Coaches' Code of Ethics Pledge

I hereby Pledge to live up to my certification as a NYSCA Coach by following the NYSCA Coaches' Code of Ethics Pledge

I will place the emotional and physical well being of my players ahead of any personal desire to win.

I will remember to treat each player as an individual, remembering the large spread of emotional and physical development for the same age group.

I will do my very best to provide a safe playing situation for my players.

I promise to review and practice the necessary first-aid principles needed to treat injuries of my players.

I will do my best to organize practices that are fun and challenging for all my players.

I will lead by example, in demonstrating fair play and sportsmanship to all my players.

I will insure that I am knowledgeable in the rules of each sport that I coach, and that I will teach these rules to my players.

I will use coaching techniques appropriate for each of the skills that I teach.

I will remember that I am a youth coach, and that the game is for children and not adults.

National Standards for Youth Sports

#1 Proper Sports Environment

Parents must consider and carefully choose the proper sports environment for their child, including the appropriate age and development for participation, the type of sport, the rules of the sport, the age range of the participants, and the proper level of physical and emotional stress.

#2 Programs Based on the Well-Being of Children

Parents must select youth sports programs that are developed and organized to enhance the emotional, physical, social and educational well-being of children.

#3 Drug, Tobacco & Alcohol-Free Environment

Parents must encourage a drug, tobacco and alcohol-free environment for their children.

#4 Part of a Child's Life

Parents must recognizee that youth sports are only a part of a child's life.

#5 Training

Parents must insist that coaches are trained and certified.

#6 Parent's Active Role

Parents must make a serious effort to take an active role in the youth sports experience of their child providing positive support as a spectator, coach, league administrator and/or caring parent

#7 Positive Role Models

Parents must provide positive role models, exhibiting sportsmanlike behavior at games, practices, and home, while also giving positive reinforcement to their child and support to their child's coaches.

#8 Parental Commitment

Parents must demonstrate their commitment to their child's youth sports experience by annually signing the Parent's Code of Ethics Pledge.

#9 Safe Playing Situations

Parents must insist on safe playing facilities, healthful playing situations, and proper first aid applications, should the need arise.

#10 Equal Play Opportunity

Parents, coaches, and league administrators must provide equal sports play opportunity for all youth regardless of race, creed, sex, economic status or ability.

#11 Drug, Tobacco & Alcohol-Free Adults

Parents must be drug, tobacco and alcohol-free at youth league sporting events.

Parent's Code of Ethics Pledge

I hereby pledge to provide positive support, care, and encouragement for my child participating in youth sports by following this Parent's Code of Ethics Pledge.

I will encourage good sportsmanship by demonstrating positive support for all my players, coaches, and officials at every game.

I will place the emotional and physical well-being of my child ahead of my personal desire to win.

I will insist that my child play in a safe and healthy environment.

I will provide support for the coaches and officials working with my child to provide a positive, enjoyable experience for all.

I will demand a drug, alcohol and tobacco-free sports environment for my child and agree to assist by refraining from their use at all youth sports events.

I will remember that the game is for the children and not for the adults.

I will do my very best to make youth sports fun for my child.

I will ask my child to treat other players, coaches, fans and officials with respect regardless of race, sex, creed or ability.

I will promise to help my child enjoy the youth sports experience within my personal constraints by assisting with coaching, being a respectful fan, providing transportation or whatever I am capable of doing.

I will require that my child's coach be trained in the responsibilities of being a youth sports coach and that the coach upholds the NYSCA Coaches' Code of Ethics.

I will read the NYSCA National Standards for Youth Sports and do everything in my power to assist all youth sports organizations to implement and enforce them.

Players' Code of Ethics Pledge

I hereby pledge to provide a positive attitude and be responsible for my participation in Youth Sports by following this Code of Ethics:

I will encourage good sportsmanship from fellow players, coaches, officials and parents at every game and practice.

I will attend every practice and game that is reasonably possible and notify my coach if I cannot

I will expect to receive a fair and equal amount of playing time.

I will do my very best to listen and learn from my coaches.

I will treat my coaches with respect regardless of race, sex, creed or abilities and I will expect to be treated accordingly.

I deserve to play in an alcohol, tobacco and drug free environment and expect adults to respect that wish.

I will encourage my parents to be involved with my team in some capacity because it's important to me.

I will do my very best in school.

I will remember that sports is an opportunity to learn and have fun.

NYSCA
National Youth Sports
Coaches Association

About This Manual

Who Is This Manual For?

"The youth player needs a teacher, not just a coach."

This manual is for all of you moms, dads, and volunteers that give your time to teaching and developing youth athletes through an age-based recreation league which typically ranges from ages 6-13. Whether you are experienced or a first-time coach, there is a lot of planning and hard work ahead. If you are like most of us, you want to do a good job, and you know there are a lot of questions to consider. What formations are appropriate for which age groups? How many offensive plays do you teach them? Is there a common football "language" which should be used? Which blocking techniques are current and legal? How do you organize the first week of practices? What drills are both safe and effective? How do you measure results, deal with parents, motivate players, and so on and so forth?

If you are looking for help in these areas, then this manual is for you!

What's Important?

First, let me take the opportunity to tip my hat to anyone who is willing to volunteer his time to help kids play sports. It's a tremendous way to make a difference in our society, and the typical recreation leagues are organized and managed in a way which attempt to promote effective teaching. You are a special person for wanting to be involved!

"Focus on basics and positive experiences in preparing them for the next level."

The intent of this manual is to share my fifteen years of learning how to teach the game to kids in an effective way, while focusing on the things most important to the player's development at these ages. The important things include teaching young athletes to learn the basic fundamentals of the game, having fun, and developing in a way that will prepare them for the next level. Year after year and clinic after clinic, I've heard junior high and high school coaches stress how important it is for youth programs to focus on basics and positive experiences in preparing them for higher levels. Things like simplification, proper techniques, and supportive coaching styles promote a player's interest in continuing to play the game.

However, leagues depend on volunteers, and not every volunteer coach has the training or resources to know how to focus on the right things.

That's where this manual can help! Whether or not you elect to use it, always remember *that your efforts should be for the kids' sake!* You can make a tremendous difference in the kids' desire and ability to continue playing the game.

How To Use This Manual

The design is both user friendly and practical for use right on the field. A series of icons has been included to help guide you through the chapters:

 Helmets are used to highlight a different topic.

 Keys are used to indicate the techniques and/or important teaching skills.

 Numbered whistles indicate a drill is included in Chapter 10 for that particular technique. Simply flip to the chapter and locate the drill by its number.

 Anecdotes called "Learning The Hard Way" are included throughout the book to share my experiences and lessons learned. Take the time to read these if you want to avoid the same mistakes!

Each section is divided by labeled tabs, and there is an appendix on additional subject matter.

"The formula for success is keeping it simple!"

It's designed to be taken from the shelf, studied and utilized right on the practice field, with very little supplemental information required. There is no need to start from scratch, diagramming plays, outlining practice sessions, inventing drills, and planning the many other activities experienced coaches spend years developing on their own. The spiral binder allows you to flip to any page, permitting easy viewing of the written or illustrated material. You will find the minimum basic for playing the game without getting into the more sophisticated techniques required of older players. In other words, it focuses on the appropriate skills for the age group. The formula for success is keeping it simple!

In addition to instructions, it includes photos of actual players, illustrated offensive and defensive alignments, planned practice sessions and drills, all of which will help you have a successful program. It also includes a sufficient number of offensive plays appropriate for youth competition.

About This Manual

Systematic Model - "The F.A.S.T. Approach"

F.A.S.T is a simplistic, yet practical, model I've developed to help you implement an effective program resulting in a positive experience for players, parents and coaches.

The model develops a simple way to focus and teaches the right things for an effective youth athletic program, not just football...any team sport. It focuses on integrating **F**un, **A**ttitude, **S**kills and **T**eamwork in a balanced approach to both practices and games. It provides activities and guidelines for each of the elements. Finally, It becomes an instinctive symbol coaches, players and family can relate to.

A reference chart called "The F.A.S.T. Checklist" is also included.

Simplified Teaching Techniques

Simplified teaching techniques are offered through the use of pictorial sketches for offensive plays, color coding for formations play names instead of numbering schemes, and other suggestions. It improves the ability of younger players to understand and learn formations and plays, without having to learn complex numbering schemes.

It provides a gradual transition to the traditional X's and O's method of learning higher level football.

Offensive and Defensive Position Skills

Fundamental techniques are provided for each offensive and defensive position. There is emphasis on footwork, stances, use of the hands/arms, body position, etc.

Fundamentals of safe and effective tackling are discussed in detail. A separate chapter includes an abundance of proved individual and team drills.

Offensive and Defensive Strategies

A basic orientation to the theories is provided, including illustrations of various formations for both offense and defense. Common terms are provided; these will help players relate as they move on year to year, and play for different coaches and at higher levels.

Finally, tips are provided on how to develop your own personal strategy for offense and defense.

About This Manual

Message To The Parents

In teamwork, everyone has a role, including the parents. I have included my thoughts for parents to consider, such as expectations, understanding the coach's role, and building self-esteem. In other words, getting involved in the "right" way.

Offensive Playbook

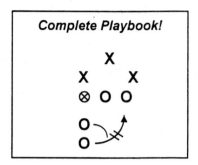

Complete Playbook!

At the end of the manual is a suggested offensive play book of selected plays from the commonly used youth formations: T, Wing-T, I, and Power-I. Each formation includes basic run plays inside, outside, off-tackle, traps, and counters.

Pass plays include both the play action and drop-back pass. Each play has a double-sided page design with **X's and O's** on one side, and the same play animated with players, for the younger ones on the flip side. The choice is yours!

Don't worry, if it doesn't satisfy your needs, there's a blank page included you can use with a dry erase pen to create your own plays.

The Kicking Game

Don't forget the kicking game, you can't overlook it. This section includes fundamentals of the center snap, including the point-after attempt. Basic punting and kick-off skills are included, along with formations for both phases of the game.

Practice Schedules

A separate section is dedicated to the first full week of practice, complete with drills, and warm-up techniques illustrated with photos.

Basic Football Rules

You can't teach the game without understanding "why the yellow flags fly." The most common rule infractions and associated penalties are included in the appendix.

Safety

The most important aspect of the program is player safety. Included in this manual is a "Do's and Don'ts" checklist prepared specifically for football by the American Red Cross.

Conclusion

"Your own personal experiences in playing the game or just your recollection of how it should be played may not be appropriate for developing today's youth athletes"

This concludes a brief introduction to this manual. I hope you will discover that it meets your fundamental needs in developing and implementing a youth football program. In case you are called upon to coach other sports, you'll see that the "F.A.S.T." approach applies universally to them, as well. Whether you use my approach, your own or another, please remember, this game is for the players. Your personal experiences in playing the game, or just your recollection of how it should be played, may not be appropriate for developing today's youth athletes. This is a big responsibility, and playing the game should be a positive experience for the players, one they will always associate with you. Good luck, and thanks for volunteering your time!

F.A.S.T.
APPROACH

The F.A.S.T. Approach To Teaching Youth Football

What Is The F.A.S.T. Approach?

"It's a "how to" approach for both practices and games."

F.A.S.T. is a model for implementing a successful athletic program. Models are commonly used in business to help work teams easily identify with what the organization is trying to accomplish, and how each person contributes to the success. It's a simple method to stay focused on what's important; it works in athletics, just as it does in business. My method can help coaches, players and parents to continuously relate to the program's objectives. It's a "how to" approach for both practices and games.

F.A.S.T. stands for Fun, Attitude, Skills, and Teamwork. When you put it in perspective, these are the areas in which you want to develop the youth athlete. ***The four elements are interdependent parts of the whole method, as illustrated by the symbol.*** All you have to do is see that each element is integrated into your weekly activities. Obviously, at any point in the season, one element will require more emphasis than the others. You don't have to achieve an equal balance each day or each week, for that matter. However, at the end of each week, you should be able to recap how each of the four elements were part of the activities. Give it a try. It's simple, yet practical and effective!

Simply thinking and referring to the acronym before, during and after practices and games will force you to stay on target in planning and executing all your activities. If you reinforce it, after two or three weeks it will become instinctive in your teaching. The Logo also becomes a physical symbol with which the whole team can identify. Print it on shirts and handouts, use it as a supplemental decal for your helmet, etc. I authorize and encourage you to use it for this purpose! Make it an integral part of your on-going dialogue. See how fast it catches on!

Coach Ray's Personal Philosophy

Before we get into details of the "how to" of F.A.S.T., let me share some background, and my opinion on how to develop youth players. I have been coaching youth sports for many years and it's my all time favorite hobby. I've used a variety of approaches to develop the players, and, like most, I've made some mistakes along the way. I've coached ages 6 - 14 in several different sports, and I have learned that my job as a youth coach is to teach and build character, and ensure they get the development needed to keep playing the game. However, to do that you need to have a plan. That's where F.A.S.T. comes into play; it provides me a method and keeps me focused.

The F.A.S.T. Approach To Teaching Youth Football

Learning The Hard Way: "The Case of All Work and No Play!"

 It was in the late 1970's. Although I had virtually no coaching experience, I was talked into head coaching a 13/14 year old age-group, because no one else had the time. I didn't even have any children, but my good friend was age-group director, and he persuaded me to do it. Fortunately I discovered a top-notch assistant, plus the dads turned out to be exceptional volunteers. We had fun, learned a great deal, and, in many ways, the program was successful. On the other hand, there were some things I could have done much better! For example, I focused more on work than fun!

"I thought I had to be like those who had taught me!"

Unfortunately, I relied upon my experience as a high school player (more than 15 years removed), and my background of discipline training from the Marine Corps. When I took the field, I thought I had to be like those who had taught me. "Do what I say", "That's not good enough," "Run some more," "Why can't you guys get it right," etc. I didn't realize at the time, but my aggressive style slowed the level of learning, and reduced the amount of fun we should have enjoyed.

"Would they be happy to see me today?"

Fortunately, the kids were old enough to take it in stride, and most of them did just that. At least half of them progressed to play at the high school level. However, I'll always wonder if it was a positive experience for all of the players. Did I work them too hard? Did I fail to teach some of them the right skills? Did they all feel good about themselves? Do some of them have a bad memory? Did I make the effort to understand what was important to them? Finally, would they be happy to see me today?

I have continued to learn and grow from my mistakes, and now I understand that coaching youth sports really is *"For Kid's Sake!"* Competition will get tougher soon enough, so build a solid foundation to help them succeed when they get to that level.

"You never forget the coaches in your life"

Once again, teaching youth sports is my hobby, and I get a great deal of personal satisfaction by feeling I have made a difference in developing a player. However, I want to do it the right way. Hopefully, my reward will be that they will remember me for a long time in a very positive way. Someone once said: "You never forget the coaches in your life." After I thought about it, I began to remember almost all of those who taught me. Can you remember your coaches?

Now, enough about my philosophy, let's learn about how to implement F.A.

Following are guidelines and activities for your use in integrating each of the four elements into your program. Don't worry, there is an easy to use check-list which summarizes everything for you, and it is included at the end of the chapter.

Fun

Face it, if an athlete is not having fun, there are many alternatives from which to choose. Many high school coaches will tell you there are fewer players trying out for football than in past years. They speculate that somewhere along the way, they are being "burned out," having a bad experience, or simply choosing a less demanding form of fun and competition. When they are young, having fun is the key motivation factor. Here are some ways I incorporate fun into my programs:

- *Keep players **participating** as much as possible. Avoid standing around waiting to participate in a drill. When not participating, dedicate another coach to work with them on techniques. Keep them moving and involved throughout the practice.*

- *Ensure adequate **playing time** during games and scrimmages. When not playing, have a dedicated coach reviewing responsibilities and techniques, in preparation for entering the game.*

- ***Vary** practice **routines** with different warm-ups, drills, and conditioning. Run sprints early or during practice, rather than always at the end.*

- *Introduce **"fun drills"** as often as **practical;** it makes a tremendous difference. Following are some "fun drills" my teams enjoy:*

<u>Tag Sprint.</u> This is the same as regular sprints, but includes competition, fun, and push-ups for the "tagged." Line-up 5 to 6 players, side by side. The sprints should be 30 to 40 yard distances. Coach stands behind the players, starts them sprinting, then calls out one of their names. Whoever is called must tag one of the other runners before crossing the finish line. The player tagged has to do pushups after crossing the line. Kids of all age groups love this one, plus it's still the same old running sprints. The fun and competition takes the dread out of running them!

<u>Rock-around-the-clock</u>. Outline a circle 20 to 30 feet in diameter and position players at intervals on the perimeter of the circle, such as the quarter hours of a clock. Instruct which direction to run, clockwise or counter clockwise. On the coaches command, players chase the one in front of them, attempting to tag him. Any player who gets tagged stays on the circle until only one is left. Make sure to run them according to ability, otherwise, it becomes unfair. You can use cones to form the circle.

The F.A.S.T. Approach To Teaching Youth Football

Fun, *continued*

Tug of war. Use a 2 inch or larger diameter cotton rope and have the players compete in this traditional game. Lie a blocking dummy flat on the ground, with ends pointed outward from the rope. As a player is pulled across the dummy, he is out. Position coaches at each end of the dummy for safety. Don't let them fall on each other and get hurt! This is an excellent way to end up a practice session and a great way to develop camaraderie with an opponent following a scrimmage.

Relay races. Run relays by executing hand-offs, or recovering fumbles. This combines both fun and technique development.

Team Run. Align your players in 3 columns and in rows side by side, with sufficient distance between them. Position coaches at the point, the side and the rear of the formation. Begin by walking or running half speed to keep the players aligned. Make up some team songs and have the players join during certain parts of the cadence. It can build fitness and instill team spirit. ***Don't knock it until you've tried it!***

Invent your own "fun drills," but make sure the objective includes competition and some form of aerobic activity.

Attitude

Individual and team development will be influenced significantly by the attitudes of all the players. When any team first comes together, it's only natural there will be a wide range of attitudes towards you, the other team members, and the objectives you set out to accomplish. Your job is to help individual players learn to align their personal attitudes with the team objectives. This will always be one of the greatest challenges any coach has to manage. The F.A.S.T. approach emphasizes developing attitudes both on and off the field. A coach quickly becomes a role model, and can significantly influence the values and beliefs of the players. It is an opportunity which should not be overlooked...it's called "making a difference."

Use the following techniques to develop and align attitudes.

"Make sure to administer the rules consistently!"

 Establish fair and reasonable ground rules by which all players have to adhere. Three or four key rules are generally sufficient for all activities. Explain the importance of each rule and get each player to agree that it is fair, and that a violation of the rule may result in some type of constructive reprimand, such as sitting out of participation. Make sure to administer the rules consistently! Following are basic Ground Rules I propose to my players:

Attitude, *continued*

Ground Rule # 1. Head coaches and staff are authorities on the field at all times. All players will respect and respond to each of them. <u>There are no exceptions</u>.

Ground Rule #2. When coaches and staff are instructing or informing, all <u>heads</u> will be <u>up,</u> and <u>eyes</u> <u>locked</u> onto the teacher.

Ground Rule #3. Attendance is a must, and absences are <u>required to be cleared</u> through the head coach, or designated staff member.

"Always ask your players, "Was that your best effort?"

Develop the desire to compete. One of the most important tasks you will have all season is to instill the desire to compete. Athletic competition is about out-performing the opponent. Remind players of this simple concept and teach them that it is okay to lose, as long as they have done their best. Doing their best requires discipline, skill development, practice repetition, and on-going encouragement. Always ask your players, "Was that your best effort?" Long after the program has ended, your players should remember, "Do your best and never quit; if so, you will always be a winner."

Develop Sportsmanship. Sportsmanship is appropriate behavior toward opponents, officials, coaches, fans and all others involved in the game. Appropriate behaviors include congratulating opponents, helping players to their feet and recognizing a good effort, displaying respect to an official's call, etc. There is no excuse for a player to taunt an opponent, smart-off to coaches and officials, or display a child-like tantrum following a defeat. By the way, it's also subject to a 15 yard penalty!

Give real-time positive feedback to all players. Every player is going to do something well each practice and deserves the positive reinforcement, either by a coach and / or the whole team.

Teach Respect for Diversity. Most teams will be a combination of players from different backgrounds. Some may be minority, more skilled or less skilled than others, come from different income families, different religious backgrounds, etc. Contrary to some people's perceptions, diversity improves a team's ability to be successful. Regardless of personal biases, players must learn to value and respect diversity. **It's never permissible for players to criticize or ridicule one of their teammates**. It is up to the coach to reinforce this valuable learning.

Attitude, *continued*

"The "Coaches Box" *concept is an opportunity to shape values and beliefs!"*

 Require Personal and Team Goals. Early in the season work with players to establish both personal and team goals. Write them down and follow-up as the season progresses.

 Make time for the *"Coach's Box"* concept. The personal development of Values and Beliefs is an integral part of becoming an athlete, and can be significantly influenced by the coaches. The "coach's box" is a technique I've used successfully. It involves the players, coaches and parents. Once per week my team has a post-practice session (approx. 30 minutes). Following practice, team moms and dads provide refreshments and/or treats. After a few minutes of fun and socializing, players and parents gather around the coach for a serious discussion on personal and citizenship-type behaviors expected of athletes. It is intended to be an interactive discussion, at which time the players share their views and understanding on a selected topic. Following are some suggested topics that I have used effectively. <u>This works like magic!</u>

Suggested Topics:

The Importance Of Reading. Discuss how this applies to growing and learning in all aspects of life, including sports. Following the discussion, you may wish to hand out a monthly edition of some popular sports publication, i.e. *Sports Illustrated For Kids*

Respect In The Home And The Classroom. Discuss why respect is an expectation of all children, especially the youth athlete, because others look up to them.

Kids Against Drugs. Many officials are available for this discussion. Athletes have the ability to influence others; encourage them to be leaders, not followers.

Learning To Value Diversity. Teamwork is the greatest opportunity to learn, understand and value how everyone has something to offer, regardless of race, creed, religious background, etc. It's easier to learn it as a child, so emphasize it!

Personal Goal Setting. Confidence, gratification and feelings of self-worth are extremely critical to kids. Don't pass up the opportunity to help them understand how this helps them to grow in sports, school and every other aspect of their life. Accomplishing a goal builds self confidence.

Winning And Losing. What does it really mean and how do you deal with it, particularly as a youth athlete.

Select other values and actions which will help develop an appropriate attitude toward those things important in life.

The F.A.S.T. Approach To Teaching Youth Football

Skills

Developing basic skills requires the teaching of proven techniques, together with drills and repetition. Following is a minimum list of techniques each player should develop, regardless of the position played. Each technique is covered in a separate chapter and drills are contained in a separate chapter.

Teach these skills and use them as a checklist in evaluating your players' progress and development.

- **Stance and Balance.** The 3 and 4 point down stances utilize angles and acceleration to physically move an opponent. The "breakdown," or "ready" position, is an upright stance used by different positions and in different situations.

- **Blocking.** Blocking is taught with both the Shoulder and Hands technique. Age and ability will generally determine on an individual basis which technique is most effective. The target areas for blocking are the sternum, or upper body, and the waist or belt buckle. <u>However, blocking below the waist is only permitted by certain positions within a certain area of the playing field.</u>

- **Selected Blocks.** Other fundamental blocks include the Cross/Angle, Double team, Reach/Scramble, Trap, Down-Field, and Pass Protection.

- **Movement and Footwork.** Quickness in all directions can be developed through various basic drills, such as the motion drill. The feet must be aligned properly for certain positions and stances. Movement off the ball requires knowing which foot to move first for both linemen and backs. Quarterbacks must learn drop steps and how to open the feet on hand-offs, in addition to the reverse pivot.

- **Contact.** There are various approaches for both offensive and defensive line play. I teach a 3-step approach for both. Players can learn it and remember it.

- **Tackling.** Basic rules have been implemented to reduce the risk of injury. This is one of the most important skills a player must learn. The head is always up, the neck bulled, and contact is never made to the trunk of the body with the facemask or the top of the helmet.

- **Fumble Recoveries.** Another skill which must be carefully taught in order to reduce the risk of injury. The "Dive and Fetus Position" technique is an effective and safe way to recover a fumbled football.

- **Running.** Proper use of the arms, legs, and toes can improve speed and balance.

The F.A.S.T. Approach To Teaching Youth Football

Teamwork

"Like the links in a chain!"

Players should be taught that football is a team sport in which all players have key responsibilities as teammates. Football requires eleven teammates working together, like the links in a chain!

Plan time to teach the following player responsibilities, and hold them accountable.

- Understand the basic concepts of offensive and defensive play.

- Teach that individuals don't win or lose games, teams do!

- Understand how "11" play together as one, understand the position responsibilities and how they contribute to the team's success.

- Be willing to play the position assigned by the coach.

- Always recognize and encourage teammates.

- Do the best possible, and never quit.

- Understand how the personal development goal fits with the team goal.

- Always have fun!

Learning The Hard Way: "Case of The Unevaluated Player"

It was one of those seasons in which we had a lot of players, very few assistant coaches, and minimal practice time, due to a lot of teams and limited fields on which to practice. Before I realized it, several games had passed and Johnny wasn't getting much playing time. He just didn't *seem* to have the desire and ability relative to the other kids. His parents, who had been patiently giving us the benefit of the doubt, approached me as to why he did not get to play as much as the others. Their questions were justified! "What is he doing wrong?" "What does he need to do to improve and get more playing time?" "Coach, he hasn't missed a practice." "You and the assistants don't seem to notice him during practice!" "This is not fair!"

Unfortunately, I was at a loss for specifics because I didn't have any. Like many, I became defensive because I perceived I was being attacked, and not at fault. The discussion did not end positively! After careful reflection and discussion with the other coaches, I realized we were wrong, and I was accountable!

The F.A.S.T. Approach To Teaching Youth Football

Learning The Hard Way: "Case of The Unevaluated Player," *continued*

Johnny didn't get the attention he needed because no one coach took the responsibility to ensure every player was continuously evaluated. Obviously, the moral of this experience is that you must have a plan which includes some form of periodic evaluation of the players progress, and someone has to take the responsibility to see that everyone gets adequate attention.

Included in Chapter 10 is an evaluation form I use with both the player and parents during mid-season. I know what you are thinking, that takes a great deal of time and effort, there's no way I can do all of that! You are right, It does take some effort! Trust me, it's worth it!

"Coaches, a simple rule of thumb is:
PLAN IT, DO IT, and MEASURE IT"

Finally, make time to measure your results. Coaches, a simple rule of thumb is **Plan** It, **Do** It, and **Measure** It. By the way, measuring success in youth sports is not about proving you are skilled at winning. Wins and Losses are only one of the measures of a successful program. Other measures, like fun, skill development and teamwork, are equally, or more important at these ages. If you coach for the right reasons, you will find a way to measure every aspect that is important to their development! I suggest you use the F.A.S.T. Checklist included at the end of this chapter.

Conclusion

Although the foregoing may seem quite comprehensive, it's really very basic and simple. Take the time to review the checklist under each element of the model, and measure your progress as you go. During the beginning of the season, take the time to explain the model to parents and players, and get them used to repeating the acronym F.A.S.T., and identifying with the logo. For example, coaches and parents should learn to conclude practices with "Tell me what you learned in F.A.S.T. today, this week, etc." You might even use an old familiar phrase, "Think Fast!" Coaches should ask the questions of themselves daily: "Where was the balance of F.A.S.T. in today's session?" Practice this approach to teaching and I believe you will feel as gratified as I do about the difference you are making in the player's development.

Finally, regardless of whether you utilize this model or some other method, make sure players learn fundamental skills, and have fun playing the game! Remember, you, as a coach, can make it happen!

The F.A.S.T. Approach To Teaching Youth Football

FUN	ATTITUDE	SKILLS	TEAMWORK
Put Fun Into Your Program	**Develop Right Attitudes**	**Teach Basic Skills and Evaluate Progress**	**Teach Players Responsibilities**
• Keep players participating and moving throughout practices	• Develop *Ground Rules* to live by and administer them consistently	• Teach the basic stances	• Understanding offensive and defensive concepts and formation position responsibilities
• Provide adequate playing time in practice and games	☛ Coach and Staff are authorities	☛ 3 Point, 4 Point, 2 Point (Backs)	• Be willing to play the position assigned
• Vary the routines to keep practice exciting	☛ Head and eyes always up when being instructed	☛ "Breakdown" - Learn balance and defending	• Encourage and support teammates
• Use standing around time to provide preparation	☛ Absences must be cleared	• Basic offensive blocks	• No individual wins or loses a game - it takes 11
• Add fun drills that are also skill based safe and competitive	• Develop the desire to compete	☛ Drive, Double Team, Pull, Downfield, Pass Protection	• Individual and team goals need to be aligned
☛ Tag Sprint	• Teach and insist on sportsmanship	• Use of the hands and arms in blocking and defending	• "Give your best effort and never quit"
☛ Rock Around The Clock	• Teach players the value of diversity	☛ Closed Cup / Palms Down	• Understand the rules and penalties for infractions
☛ Relay Races	• Develop personal and team goals	☛ Open Hands	• Use safe and effective drills
☛ Team Run	• Try the "Coach's Box" technique	• Footwork and movement for each position	• Measure team progress
• Help them look forward to coming to practice	• Evaluate each player's development	• Tackling fundamentals	• Make certain that safety of the players is your 1st priority!
	• "Was that your best effort?"	☛ Straight Up	• Have fun!
		☛ Angle	
		• Recovering fumbles	
		• Running techniques	
		• Give formal feedback	

For Parent's Sake!

Message From The Coach To The Parents

This manual would be incomplete if I did not take the opportunity to involve you, the parent/guardian. This is as much of an experience for you as it is for your child. I know, I've been there, and experienced it. My message to you is that it's absolutely critical for you to develop and demonstrate the appropriate level of support, while your child begins and continues this experience. You have a lot of dreams, hopes and expectations for your child to be successful. This is one of the greatest times of your life, watching your child play and grow! What you must do is make the effort to understand that success is measured by learning, and having a positive experience. Put more simply, your job is to provide them support and encouragement to do their best, have fun, and feel good about themselves. I can't tell you how many times I've seen a parent put undue pressure on a child, to the extent the player dreaded the experience! Take a look at my model, and see if that approach doesn't make more sense.

Both you and the coach have important roles, and for that reason, this chapter is dedicated to you.

Your Role vs. The Coach's Role

Coaches and parents each have a distinct role in the development of the child. All too often, coaches fail to have early season briefings on objectives, roles, practice plans and expectations. This results in parents having to speculate and develop their own perspective of the progress of their child, the team and the overall program. This situation can easily be avoided by simple up front and ongoing communication. If the coach fails to provide an orientation, for whatever reason, parents have a responsibility to approach the coach and develop an understanding.

Whether the coach is a seasoned professional or an experienced volunteer dad or mom, like many recreational coaches, they have elected to accept the responsibility as the authority, or one of the authorities, for instructing your child. As such, they deserve respect and fair treatment, especially during practices and games. A parent's negative actions or behavior toward the coach during practice or games can dramatically affect the coaches ability to effectively carry out the program. Equally important, it may impact the kids! Unfortunately, I've seen it happen all too often, when it could have been avoided. Following are some things you can do to help the coach:

- Make every attempt to attend parent orientations or periodic meetings scheduled by the coach, or another member of the staff.

- Know and adhere to the team rules regarding practice schedules, teaching objectives, and on-the-field behaviors.

Your Role vs. The Coach's Role, *continued*

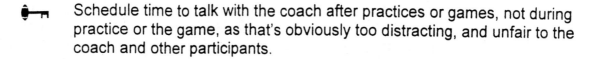 Schedule time to talk with the coach after practices or games, not during practice or the game, as that's obviously too distracting, and unfair to the coach and other participants.

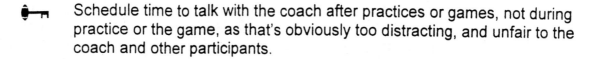 It's okay to voice your legitimate concerns or questions, but do it in a way that's non-aggressive, or challenging. Human nature being what it is, many people have a natural tendency towards "fight" or "flight" when being confronted.

Knowledge Of The Game

"When they become teenagers and "know everything," being able to relate to sports will at least be some way of having common ground!"

Your ability to relate to the sport in which your child participates makes it much easier to provide the support he or she needs to be successful.

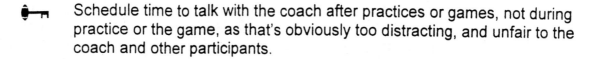 Understand the fundamentals of the game. You can do that by working through this manual and asking the coach to explain things you don't quite understand.

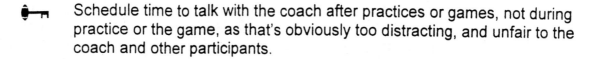 Ask the coaches to provide explanations of what techniques are being taught, why and how you can reinforce the learnings at home.

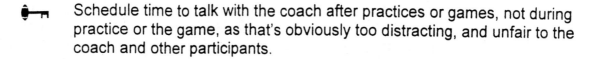 Spend quality time discussing it with your child. Trust me, when they become teenagers and "know everything," being able to relate to sports will at least be some way of having common ground!

Expectations For Success

According to the National Youth Sports Coaches Association, physical, social and emotional characteristics generally change <u>significantly</u> between the ages of six and fourteen.

It's only natural for parents to have high expectations for their child's success as an athlete. That's wonderful, provided parents can effectively manage the situations in which the player doesn't progress as expected. Keep the following in mind:

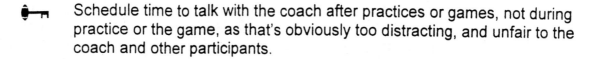 Physical abilities change over time, and often dramatically. A player who excelled at a younger age, may not have the physical attributes to compete at higher levels in junior high and high school. The reverse is also true. Many kids don't begin to excel until they hit puberty. Regardless of how and when they develop, if they aren't having a positive experience, they probably will find another alternative! This fact of life requires a lot of patience and understanding from you!

Expectations For Success, *continued*

- According to the National Youth Coaches Association, physical, social and emotional characteristics generally change <u>significantly</u> between the ages of six and fourteen. Having coached all the youth age groups, I can validate this fact. For example, I coached several kids ages 13-14 who did not have the physical size, speed or agility to compete at junior high and freshman high school levels. One to two years later they were starters for their high school team. Why? They had learned the basic skills, enjoyed playing and their physical abilities ***changed overnight***. There are many times you just never know!

- Be sure the child is in the right sports environment. If they are not having fun and learning, there may be a better alternative at that point in time. Did you ever participate in something you just didn't enjoy?

Building Self-Esteem

"No one player wins or loses the game, it's a team effort"

The coach, the players and the parents influence your child's self-esteem. You can help the coach by taking certain steps to build your child's self-esteem.

- Focus on the right objectives: having fun, learning skills, developing an attitude to compete and teamwork.

- Put "winning" in proper perspective for youth competition. It's just a game, and as long as players try their best, they are winners, regardless of the score. I'm sure most of you have seen the television commercial by the Double Arches. It's halftime, it's raining, the game is intense, and the coach is giving a pep talk to inspire the team to victory. A player interrupts and says: "Coach, can we go to McDonald's now?" I don't know about you, but I got the message!

- Provide support and understanding for individual mistakes, no one player wins or loses the game, it's a team effort.

- Reinforce the values of athletic competition as a ***sport and extracurricular activity***. Participating is a privilege that is earned only after other obligations have been satisfied, such as education and family responsibilities.

For Parent's Sake!

Sportsmanship

Parents should serve as role models on and off the field. Certain behaviors and actions exemplify sportsmanship.

- Always display respect for game officials; it's okay to disagree, but don't let players think it is okay to be disrespectful. Besides, do you really think the official is going to change his/her decision?

- Teach your player to respect the opponent. Youth sports should not be used to create ill will toward an opponent.

- Support your coach by reinforcing your player's respect for diversity. Every player from a different socio-economic background, race, religion, etc., has something to offer. If respected by <u>all</u>, diversity increases a team's chance for success.

Player Safety

Football is a game of physical contact and injuries are a possibility. However, with proper equipment and the teaching of correct techniques, it is one of the safest sports. In the September 1996 edition, *Sports Illustrated For Kids* points out that youth football is statistically safer than soccer. The reasons are primarily two-fold: youth players generally don't produce the acceleration and force to cause serious injury, and each player is covered in state of the art equipment, which is designed to protect against injury. As the parent, there are other things you can do to minimize the risks:

- Make sure your child's helmet fits properly and has a current seal certifying that the helmet meets the current National Operating Committee for Standards for Athletic Equipment (N.O.C.S.A.E.).

- Ensure all other pads fit properly, snug against the body, and not prone to slippage upon contact.

- Understand the tackle technique being taught. In the late 1970's, in order to reduce head and neck injuries, High School Federations and Colleges made it Illegal to use the facemask or top of the helmet to ram the opponent. Players should be taught in accordance with the technique outlined in this manual.

- Learn and practice minor bumps and bruises control with techniques like Rest, Ice, Compression, and Elevation (R.I.C.E.). <u>Get familiar with the American Red Cross Guidelines in the appendix</u>.

- Never take an injury too lightly; when in doubt, take your player to the doctor.

For Parent's Sake!

Learning The Hard Way: "Criticized Without Knowing Why"

 It was one of those emotional games and my players were out-performing the opponent. The opposing coach called time out, ran onto the field, and began to openly criticize one of his players. The words were something to the effect: "You're not trying, you're getting your tail kicked, etc., etc., now hit the bench." The player was embarrassed, hurt, and confused. The other players on both teams obviously had to experience some emotional feelings about what had just taken place. As I watched in dismay, my first thought was: "He didn't even tell him what he did wrong!" Can you imagine the long-lasting impression on this child's self esteem? Granted, there will come a time at a certain level of the sport that such actions may be more appropriate, but it is certainly not at the youth level! I admitted to myself that I too had occasionally been guilty of criticizing without explaining the mistake, and what they could do to improve. It's a vulnerability which can occur when things get emotional, and both coaches and parents should guard against it.

Summary

- Parents and coaches really need to communicate at the beginning of the season.

- Both parents and coaches have important roles, and each needs to understand the role of the other.

- Coaches need parents' support and involvement in helping kids adhere to the rules, learn the objectives, and focus on development.

- Parents need to be cognizant of the fact that kids' skills and abilities change throughout their childhood; be patient and focus on having fun and learning the basics.

- The more you know about the game, the better you will be able to relate to your child.

- A player's self esteem will likely be critical to continued development.

- Safety is the most important aspect of the game, and it all begins with proper fitting and authorized equipment; teaching proper techniques; being knowledgeable of injury / illness prevention; emergency preparedness and procedures.

- Everyone involved with the game has a role in promoting sportsmanship, both on and off the field.

Offensive Line Fundamentals

 ## Offensive Linemen

The key responsibilities are to execute run and pass blocking techniques against the defensive opponents, so that the offensive running backs may advance the ball toward the opponents' goal line. The skills required are proper stance, balance, use of the hands and arms, ability to move in all directions, and physical contact with the defender.

Linemen execute blocks from a down position. An effective down stance allows the body to "coil," and strike at an angle into the opponents' body. The key is to strike the opponent first, stopping forward momentum, and driving the player away from the running back's point of attack.

"Face it! If your linemen can't block, your backs can't run"

Coaches, in my opinion this is one of your top priorities. The running game is the foundation of an effective offense. Passing and other sophisticated aspects of the game are great, but they <u>typically</u> don't replace the effectiveness of a sound running game, unless your are loaded with exceptional talent. This is especially true of the youth leagues. It goes without saying, if your linemen can't block, your backs can't run. Give your linemen a good foundation including stance, footwork, and blocking with the both the hands and shoulders. Remember, prepare them to advance to next level!

 ## Stances

 3 Point. By placing one hand on the ground, three points of weight distribution are formed with the hand and two feet. Overall, this is generally the better stance from which to move laterally and straight ahead. Left handed players may need to reverse the following techniques.

Spread the feet apart, approximately the width of the shoulders, for balance. The toes may be even <u>or</u> the right foot dropped back, the left heel even with the instep of the right foot.

Offensive Line Fundamentals

Stances, *continued*

- Place the right hand down and in front of the body, with either the fingers or knuckles resting on the ground for balance. Put just enough weight to allow movement in any direction! The placement of the hand is approximately 12-14 inches from the front of the toes nearest the line of scrimmage, and anywhere from the center of the body, to the front of the right foot, depending on the individual's comfort. Rest the left arm across the left thigh.

- Try to position the back parallel to the ground, with the hips elevated slightly higher than the shoulders. The knees are bent to an angle which permits the body to squat, or "coil," for leverage. The trunk, thigh and lower leg approximate the letter Z.

"You can't hit what you can't see"

- The **head** and **neck** should be up and back, so the eyes are straight ahead. This is difficult for some of the younger players, due to the new experience of having to wear equipment. However, keep emphasizing that you can't hit what you can't see.

4 Point Stance

Both hands are on the ground to form four points of weight distribution with both feet. This stance is effective for straight ahead blocking and staying low against the defender. All 3 point fundamentals apply, <u>except</u> both hands are down and placed in line with each eye or shoulder, approximately 14-18 inches from the toes to the line of scrimmage. This stance places more of the shoulder weight over the hands, which will increase the ability to strike quicker. <u>However</u>, it may limit the quickness in lateral movement, such as required in the pull-block.

Offensive Line Fundamentals

 Center

This is the most critical position on the line of scrimmage. The position requires the same skills as other linemen, but has the additional responsibility to "snap" the ball into the hands of the quarterback, and execute the blocking assignment at the same time. Some youth leagues have rules that recognize the difficulty in developing skills at this position. For example, the rules might prohibit a defender from aligning directly over the center. This allows the center sufficient time to make the snap and attempt his blocking assignment. Without this type of rule, an aggressive defense could prevent younger, inexperienced kids from even executing the snap!

Techniques for snapping the ball may include one or both hands. I prefer the one-handed technique, but I always allow the player to choose whichever is more comfortable and effective.

- The stance fundamentals are the same as three or four point.

- Place the ball on the ground with tips pointed north and south or 12 and 6 o'clock. The laces are up and slightly rotated to the left side depending on the size of the snapper's hand. The objective is to bring the ball up and into the quarterback's hands so that the laces hit the upper hand's fingers.

- **One-handed Snap.** One hand is placed on the ball for snapping, with the other arm resting on, or outside of, the opposite thigh.

- **Two-Handed Snap.** Two hands are placed on the ball, with the right hand toward the front tip of the ball, left hand to the rear tip.

- For the front hand, in either one or two-handed techniques, the thumb of snapping hand is on the 1st, 2nd, or 3rd lace toward the front tip of the ball. The fingers are wrapped downward across the right side panels of the ball. When the hand is removed, it should be in the form of a hand shake.

- As the ball is snapped, it is rotated with the hand to the left and up with the tips pointing to the sidelines in a West to East or 9 and 3 o'clock position movement. Keep it parallel to the ground, while pulling it up into the hands of the quarterback. Quarterback's hands are placed into the "V" of the center's backside, with the top hand resting upward against the groin and buttocks.

Offensive Line Fundamentals

 ## Blocking Techniques

The two fundamental techniques are the shoulder block, and the hand block. Master the shoulder-block first, then progress to the use of the hand technique, if the players have the strength to use it. The two primary hit targets for the shoulder block are the upper body area, which is the opponents' sternum, or the lower body area, which is the opponents' waistline/belt buckle. Remember that blocking at the waistline/belt buckle can result in contact below the waist and is only permitted at the line of scrimmage, and within the "Free Blocking Zone," four yards on either side of the center and three yards on either side of the line of scrimmage.

The target area for the hand-block is upper body only, which is the breast plates of the opponents' shoulder pads.

 ## Three Step Approach To Blocking

1. **Aim and Step,** with the face mask towards the defender's belt buckle, using the rear foot, when the defender is positioned directly head-up-over. Step with the foot nearest the defender when he is positioned to either side. Aiming at the belt buckle area will help to keep positioned in front of the defender.

2. **Hit** the target area, upper sternum or belt buckle, with the opposite shoulder from the play side and *slide the head to the side of the opponent's body.* For example, if the play is to be run off the right guard's outside hip, the right guard would attempt to hit the opponent with his left shoulder and slide the head between the opponent and the ball carrier. Roll the forearms upward and extend the elbows outward with the arms parallel to the ground. The palms are facing down; the fists are clinched and knuckle to knuckle in the middle of the chest. Extending the arms in this manner provides a wider area for the defender to fight through, or around. Roll the hips forward and up on impact, so the defender is forced upright and easier to control.

3. **Drive** the defender back and away from the play by keeping the legs apart, knees bent, and constantly driving with the feet.

Offensive Line Fundamentals

 Drive Block With The Shoulder To Drive The Opponent Away From The Ball

Step with the proper foot and hit the shoulder upward into the opponent's body underneath the defenders sternum.

Contact should be made with the forearms and shoulder, simultaneously.

Slide the head to the side; extend the arms laterally with elbows out, fists together at the center of the chest and closed palms facing the ground, also known as closed-cup hand technique.

Keep the feet wide and drive the opponent with short, choppy steps. Some coaches are now beginning to advocate long strides vs. the short choppy steps for certain positions, such as the tight end. You be the judge!

Maintain contact with the opponent (Lock On) and push the defender back and away from ball carrier and to the ground. **KEEP THAT HEAD UP!**

Offensive Line Fundamentals

Drive Block With The Hands

- Aim at the sternum area just under base of the opponent's shoulder pad.

- Step out with the proper foot.

- Slam the hands upward into the target area, with palms open and fingers pointed upward.

- Keep the elbows locked, with the forearm extended at a 45 degree angle to the body.

- Keep arms inside the framework of the opponent's body, and never above the height of the opponent's shoulders.

- Push the opponent up and away from the ball carrier. The blocker may be able to drive the opponent on his back, if initial slam is upward with enough force.

- Maintain contact with the opponent (lock on) and push the defender away from the ball carrier. If the defender offers too much resistance, throw the shoulder into his upper body, and slide the head to the side!

Offensive Line Fundamentals

 ## Scramble/Reach-Block - To Immobilize Opponents Legs And Prevent Lateral Pursuit

- Fire and hit into the outside of the thigh, with the shoulder opposite the play side only if block occurs within "Free Block Zone".

- Keep the head up and neck pulled back.

- Drop one, or both hands, to the ground for stability.

- Keep the feet wide and use choppy steps.

- Use thigh if opponent attempts to slide off the shoulder pad and down the side of the body.

 ## Double Team Block - Two Offensive Against One Defender Using Either A Straight Shoulder Drive Block Method Or A Post and Pivot Method

- In the straight shoulder method, blockers both step with inside foot and bring hips together to form a wedge.

- Post and Pivot: One blocker serves as a **Post** by hitting upper target area to upright the defender. **Pivot** blocker angle blocks on the hip area and drives the defender away from the ball.

- The Post Man will hit straight forward and the Pivot Man will have his head on the playside of defender's body.

Offensive Line Fundamentals

Pull Or Trap Block - Used To Block A Penetrating Defender By Surprise

- The blocker begins from the down three point stance.

- The blocker should maintain a straight-ahead stance and avoid leaning or pointing, which may tip the defender that a pull technique is going to be executed.

- Step back and laterally with the pull direction foot. The pull foot opens toward the sideline.

- Jerk the pull side elbow backwards with a hard thrust to help the body turn laterally.

- Run laterally towards the defender and hit the defender, using the shoulder nearest the backfield to kick the defender outward. Use the opposite shoulder to kick inward.

- Drive through the defender upon contact, and drive him onto the ground. As the defender falls to the ground, the blocker should continue by falling on top of him and covering until the runner gets past.

Down-Field Block - Used To Lead The Running Back To The Sidelines And/Or Into The Defender's Secondary

- During the running approach, take aim at the defender's jersey number on the side the block is intended, keep the facemask crossbar constantly on the target.

- Dip the hips just before making contact with the defender.

- Use the shoulder-block and cupped hands technique, thrusting up into the defender. Slide the facemask off the side.

- Maintain contact, take the defender to the ground and cover him.

Offensive Line Fundamentals

 ## Pass Blocking

The youth passing game is one of the most difficult techniques to execute and is often ineffective because:

1. Younger quarterbacks need more time to set up and locate the appropriate receiver.

2. Most of the teaching and development time is needed on other basics such as stance and fundamentals of run blocking.

3. Defenses will generally rush the offense with six to seven players.

4. Good pass blocking takes a great deal of practice and repetition to perfect.

"The keys are to use simple pass plays, throw for less than ten yards, and teach simple Pass Blocking techniques"

This doesn't mean you shouldn't teach and include it in your game plan. In fact, I recommend your strategy include at least one to two basic pass plays, even at the youngest of the age groups. The keys are to use simple pass plays, throw for less than ten yards, and teach simple Pass Blocking techniques. There are two blocking techniques in protecting the pass play; one for Play-Action passes, and one for Drop-Back passes. I recommend the younger ages learn the traditional play action, which is a combination shoulder and hand-block used to stop defender's initial forward progress, and then prevent the defender from penetrating into the backfield. Older players should obviously learn both methods. Each requires different techniques. The Play Action is intended to influence the defense that a running play is in progress, before they realize the quarterback intends to pass. The Drop-Back is obvious to the defense from the snap, because they see the quarterback setting up with drop steps to throw the forward pass.

 ## Play Action Blocking Technique

- The Blocker takes <u>one</u> step forward with nearest foot toward the defender's path, and executes upper body shoulder-block to stop initial charge by standing up the defender. **Caution - an offensive lineman may not cross the neutral zone until the forward pass is thrown beyond the neutral zone.**

- When the blocker hits the defender, his back should be arched, feet shoulder width apart, head up, and body locked onto the defender.

- As defender charges, the blocker stays locked onto him, fighting against the resistance with hands up against sternum area, arms at 45 degree angle and inside the frame of the body.

Offensive Line Fundamentals

⌐ Action Blocking Technique, *continued*

- The blocker will have to be able to move laterally to stay locked onto, and in front of the defender, driving him opposite from the quarterback's movement. He also has to be prepared to stay locked onto, if the defender executes a reverse spin move. The blocker should never cross his feet, or he will lose his ability to maintain position and balance.

Drop Back Blocking Technique

- The blocker retreats two steps, and takes a breakdown position (feet shoulder width apart, legs and hips down, arms in front of body, ready for impact).

- As defender rushes, blocker uses open hand technique to stop opponent's forward progress. This is done by a hard hand-slam to the sternum in an upward motion, to attempt to upright the defender.

- Blocker has to move laterally to stay locked onto, and in front of the defender, while fighting against the resistance, and forcing the defender away from the quarterback's set up position.

Linemen "Blocking Rules"

"He is not where he is supposed to be, so what do I do now?"

The various blocks we have just reviewed are not difficult to teach or learn, but they do require practicing with repetition, repetition and more repetition. However, in order to be effective, the coach must consider two other critical elements:

1. Defenders are not going to stand still and allow themselves to be blocked. In fact, defensive players typically have less complicated responsibilities, thus, attacking with reckless abandon.

2. When your blocker approaches the line of scrimmage, he will often find the defense has changed their alignment, and moved into different positions. Suddenly, the offensive lineman thinks to himself; "He is not where he is supposed to be, so what do I do now?"

Coaches have developed a way to adjust for this type of situation; they've developed rules to follow. At the higher levels of the game, particularly in high school and college, these rules can get very comprehensive and generally provide a solution to any type of defensive change in alignment. In youth football, you must keep it simple, and cannot expect the kids to understand and react to very many situation changes. However, there are some simple rules they can remember which should help them.

Offensive Line Fundamentals

I Recommend You Teach The Following For The Playside Guard, Tackle And End: "On, Inside, and Nearest"

1. **"On."** If a defender is aligned directly on/over you, he is the first priority to be blocked. This includes a linebacker, who is typically 2-3 yards off the line of scrimmage.

2. **"Inside."** If a defender is not aligned directly over you, then block the defender aligned in the inside gap towards the center. You may wish to adjust this to **"outside"** or **"playside,"** depending on the defenses you encounter!

3. **"Nearest."** If the defender is not aligned directly over you or in the inside gap, block the nearest linebacker.

Many coaches prefer to teach "Inside" as the first priority. Regardless of your choice, keep it simple, so they grasp the basic concept of the need for blocking rules. If your linemen can follow these three basic rules, your play still has a probability of success. The reason is that your blocker will at least be attacking a potential tackler, rather than standing around in a state of confusion.

Learning The Hard Way: "The Case Of Blaming Players For Your Assumptions"

It was one of my famous half-time speeches, and I was criticizing the offensive line for failing to block the defenders. After all, my quarterback and running backs had their timing down flawlessly, and my play design was sure to work, if everyone did his job. One of the linemen took a deep breath of courage and stated: "Coach, my man keeps moving to both sides, and I don't know which way to block him." My offensive line coach, all 6' 4" 250 lbs. and former collegiate "junk yard dog," one of the best youth volunteer coaches ever to teach kids jumped in and exclaimed: "I've told you guys over and over, it's On, Inside and Near; why can't you remember that?" Suddenly, we noticed blank stares. It was obvious, we had spouted the rules, but failed to verify the fact that our players really understood.

We went back to the drawing boards and corrected our failings, by ensuring our players understood the techniques we were attempting to teach. Since that time, I can't count the number of incidents I've observed coaches falling into the same trap. The moral of the story is: don't assume they understand!

Stop and think about the manner in which you instruct certain fundamentals. For example, If your style is such that it intimidates, do you really think the kids are going to stand up and say: "I don't understand?" Take the time to teach and evaluate what each player has learned! That's our job, plus it will definitely impact your probability for success.

Offensive Line Fundamentals

Summary Key Fundamentals

Stance:

- Block from a three point stance for straight ahead, and lateral movement.

- Block from the four point stance to block straight ahead and low.

- Keep the feet shoulder width apart, with toes pointed straight ahead.

- Don't worry about a perfect stance as long as the player has balance and can spring out of the position.

- Keep the head and eyes up at all times.

Blocking:

- Use the three step approach of Step, Hit, and Drive.

- Target area is the upper sternum, or the waistline/belt buckle of the defender.

- Block with the shoulder, hands, or hip, accelerating from the stance, hitting the opponent before he has a chance to attack.

- Keep the legs shoulder width apart, and the knees bent; use the upper leg strength to push and drive the opponent away from the ball.

- Position the head between the defender and the running back's point of attack.

- The target area for traps, double-team and pull blocks, is the hip and side area.

- When blocking, never cross the feet.

- Remember, blocking below the waist is only permitted in the "Free Blocking Zone."

- Pass blocking involves different techniques for the play-action and the drop-back passes. Begin instruction for play action, and progress to the drop-back technique. Teach players not to cross into the neutral zone on pass blocking.

- The blocking rules for linemen are: "On, Inside and Nearest." Adjust the rules if you need to, but keep them simple at this level!

Running Back and Receiver Skills

Running Backs

Running backs should demonstrate the ability to perform more skills than any other position on the field. They have to receive hand-offs, run with speed and aggressiveness inside and outside, run block, pass block, and receive a forward pass. They cannot be tentative about physical contact, and must have the mental concentration to know all offensive schemes and strategies. The quarterback is typically the running back with the most overall skills, speed, leadership, knowledge of the game, and the ability to pass and run. On the other hand, many youth offenses utilize such talent at the tailback position, since passing tends to be less emphasized than at older levels.

Stances

Running backs can begin out of the three point or the upright two point according to the coach's personal philosophy and preference of the runner. Each stance provides certain advantages.

3-Point

- Execute the same fundamentals as for lineman.

- Keep the toes straight ahead, with heels slightly elevated and weight on the balls of the feet.

- This provides straight ahead acceleration for quick type running plays.

- The runner is more difficult to spot by the defenders when in a down stance, versus the upright stance.

2-Point

- The feet are spread shoulder-width apart.

- The toes are even for quick acceleration to either side. If preferred, one foot may be dropped slightly back in the heel to instep method.

- The toes should be pointed North/South, with the heels slightly raised and the weight on the balls of the feet.

- The knees are bent just enough to drop the buttocks to a semi- squat.

- The back is straight, with the head up and eyes forward to allow scanning the defense.

- The hands are placed on the top of the thigh pads, with fingers pointing to the ground.

Running Back and Receiver Skills

 Receiving The Hand-Off

"Runners should approach the hand-off with eyes focused on the point of attack, NOT the quarterback, or the ball."

Raise the arm nearest to the quarterback to chest height and bend the elbow, so that the forearm stretches horizontally across the top of the jersey numbers and parallel to the ground. The palm of the hand is facing the ground and the fingers are spread, flexed, and pointed away from the quarterback.

Place the other arm horizontally across the bottom of the numbers, or slightly lower, if comfortable, and parallel to the ground! The palm should be up with the fingers spread, flexed, and pointed towards the quarterback.

If these arm positions are reversed, there is a high risk the ball may be knocked loose from the quarterback's hands from contact with the bicep area of the runner's arm.

Runners should approach the hand-off with eyes focused on the point of attack, NOT the quarterback, or the ball.

As the ball is placed into the pocket, the arms should close like a vise with hands grasping the tips of the ball.

Accept the ball from the quarterback, don't try to take it.

Both arms should be used to protect the ball, as the back begins to move through the neutral zone.

The bottom arm will be used to carry the ball after breaking across the neutral zone.

Running Back and Receiver Skills

 ## Fake Hand-Off

"Continue running through the point of attack and swing the elbows from side to side, "Rocking the Baby"

- The runner forms the same pocket, as if he were actually receiving the ball.

- Run to the point of attack, with the body leaning forward.

- As quarterback pulls the ball back out of the pocket, close the arms by grabbing the elbows and bend the upper body over the arms, to give the appearance the ball has been handed off.

- Continue running through the point of attack and swing the elbows from side to side, "Rocking the Baby."

 ## Receiving The Toss or Pitchout

"Look it into the hands"

- Bring the arms and hands to chest height as the run begins.

- The palms are facing the quarterback, with fingers up and thumbs pointed inward.

- As the ball is released, lock the eyes onto ball until it is in the hands and grasped, "look it into the hands."

- If the toss is low, fan the hands outward and down, with fingers pointing to ground and thumbs to the outside.

- After "looking it into the hands," tuck the ball up against the rib cage with the arm closest to your own goal line.

Running Back and Receiver Skills

Carrying The Ball - The 3 P.O.P. Method (3 Points of Pressure)

The 3 P.O.P. is a method to help runners keep defenders from knocking the ball loose during the run. It involves putting pressure on the ball in three different areas, to keep it held tightly against the body. The use of all three pressure points will provide sufficient protection in the open field run.

The first point of pressure is applied to the front end of the ball. The carrying arm hand is clasped over the front end of the ball, with the tip in between the index, middle finger and the thumb, and other fingers are wrapped around the tip end. The ball is pulled back, up, and into the "V," or wedge of the armpit.

The second point of pressure is applied to the outside of the ball. The forearm is positioned along the lower panel of the ball, and used to hold the ball firmly against the rib cage. The elbow covers and protects the rear tip.

The third point of pressure is applied to the top side of the ball. The "V," or wedge of the armpit, helps prevent the ball from being dislodged on contact from the underside.

When running into multiple defenders, rotate the ball toward the mid-section, and place the free hand on top of the ball, to provide complete covering with the trunk of the body.

Running Techniques

"Keep the head up at all times!"

To The Line of Scrimmage

Step with the foot nearest the point of attack.

Keep the head up at all times!

Square the shoulders to the LOS.

Run straight to the hole on an inside dive. Remember the "shortest distance between two points" rule.

Keep the knees slightly bent, and the torso forward.

Running Back and Receiver Skills

To The Line Of Scrimmage, *continued*

- Protect the ball with top hand among multiple defenders. In a one-on-one contact situation, use the free arm and shoulder to repel the defender.

- Kick the knees upward to keep the defender's arms from wrapping around the legs.

- Teach the age old saying, "Run through, not to - daylight." This means the back should learn to spot the openings, whether wide or narrow, and be determined to <u>get</u> <u>through</u> <u>it</u>! Teach your runners to condition their mindset, so that they always try to get beyond the opening.

Laterally To The Sidelines

- Use a cross-over step to the sideline, or open laterally with the outside foot.

- Keep head and eyes angled to North/South, looking for the open lane.

- Manage the speed until ready to make a cut.

- Use a cross-over step to square the shoulders to line of scrimmage and begin North/South running by accelerating to full speed.

Open Field

- Push off the back foot, driving the knee forward.

- Run on the toes, keeping the upper torso slightly forward.

- Ball hand rotates back and forth from the rib to breast area.

- Rotate the free arm back and forth, straight at the side in a "hammer motion," not across the body.

- Run under control when executing evasive moves.

- Run low and full speed ahead when needing to take on the defender(s) straight up.

- To evade the defender with a **Side Step,** plant the pivot foot and push off to the opposite side.

- To use the **Spin Maneuver,** lower the free shoulder and arm into the defender and reverse spin by thrusting the ball carrying arm out and away from the defender's body.

Open Field, *continued*

   To use the **Stiff Arm,** straighten the free arm and lock the elbow. Slam the defender on the shoulder pad in attempt to stop momentum and push him off balance. This maneuver should be executed at the split second before impact. If it is executed too soon, the defender may grab the runner by the arm.

 Quarterback

Receiving The Snap From The Center

Stand behind the center, with the feet shoulder-width apart and the weight on the balls of the feet.

Bend the knees slightly and dip the hips slightly, as well. Bend the torso slightly forward so that the hands and arms will extend naturally under the center's buttocks, in preparation for the snap.

Keep the head up so that the eyes are focused on the defensive alignment.

Place the throwing hand underneath the center and press firmly up against the buttocks with the fingers spread, slightly flexed, and pointed North/South. The palm is facing downward. Keep the pressure on the buttocks so the center will know where to hit with the snap.

Place the bottom hand so that the heel of the palm meets the heel of the top hand's palm to form a "V." The bottom hand's thumb is placed against the top hand's thumb in an off-set position. This is done by positioning the bottom hand's middle thumb knuckle into the groove just beneath the top hand's middle thumb knuckle. This helps to form a natural seal when the ball is snapped into the "V" configuration of the hands.

The hands and arms should give slightly forward as the center snaps and steps forward from his stance. This will help minimize fumbles during the exchange. In the same continuous motion, pull the ball back and up into the area around the naval and prepare to step.

Running Back and Receiver Skills

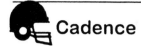 Cadence

---

*Tip - younger players respond more effectively to simple
and consistent counts!*

- Cadences are critical to getting the offensive linemen to accelerate from the stance and hit the defenders before they have a chance to fire out.

- Variations typically range from a single count, to a double or triple count.

- Variations can be used to fool the defense. If the defense becomes conditioned to the offense moving on a certain count, they tend to want to move on the same count each time. Varying the count may cause them to "jump offsides." However, good defenses are trained to avoid that mistake by learning to move on offensive player movement only.

- Sample Cadences include:

    - Ready Set - Down - Hut, Hut,
    - Get set - Hut one, Hut two,
    - Ready Down - Hike
    - Set - Get Down - Hit (My favorite recently taught to me by a Junior Varsity Coach)

- An offensive play may begin with the following typical sequence. On the first count, the players place their hands, or forearms, on their thighs and bend over; on the second count, the players put their down hand on the ground and hold motionless (can't move after this); on the next sound(s) as determined in the huddle, they step and fire out at the defenders.

- Use something <u>simple</u> and <u>rhythmic</u> that players will respond to instinctively, your choice!

- *Tip - younger players respond more effectively to simple and consistent counts!*

 Footwork And Ball Handling For The Quarterback

- As the ball is pulled from the center, it is placed into the belly around the naval, with elbows held in against the sides. Keep it in this position until ready to hand off. This is the safest technique to prevent defenders from reaching and knocking the ball loose, as the quarterback attempts to hand off.

Footwork And Ball Handling For The Quarterback, *continued*

- For hand-offs or tosses, the first step is either an open step to the play side, or a reverse pivot to the play side. For passing, the first step is back, followed by crossover steps, backpedaling, or rolling out.

- **CLOCK TECHNIQUE**: This is a good method for easy learning and execution!

  Assume a clock circles the QB and/or Running Back's feet with 12 directly ahead, and 6 directly to the rear.

  The quarterback's foot can move to the clock's hour for selected running plays. For example, he may open the foot to 3 o'clock for hand-offs to quick running plays into the right side, or open to 9 o'clock for the same on the left side of the line. He may open to 5 o'clock to gain depth in the backfield for off tackle play on the right side, or 7 for the left side. 5 or 7 o'clock can also be used for the roll out pass, while stepping to the 6 can be used for drop-back passes and draw plays.

  For the drop-back pass the first step is generally to 5 or 6 o'clock. The next step can be a cross-over with the opposite foot, and be continued for 3, 5, or 7 steps back to a point where he sets up and executes the throw. For backpedaling, the first step can be at 5 or 6 with the lead foot, followed by the opposite foot for a similar number of steps to the desired depth. I recommend the crossover if it's going to be a drop back, unless the quarterback is exceptionally quick, and can throw while backpedaling.

- The REVERSE PIVOT is often effective for additional leverage on toss sweeps and pitchouts, or deception on inside running plays. The pivot foot is on the side of the pitch, or hand-off; pivot is made on the ball of the foot with the opposite leg swinging around toward the running back. On the toss, the arms are swung from hip and outstretched, parallel to each other, with the thumbs facing down after release of the ball. Keeping the thumbs down will make the ball easier to catch, by keeping it from turning end-over-end. The ball will tend to "float" in the air, allowing the runner to grasp it firmly and quickly.

 **Passing**

Grip:

- Place the joint nearest to the tip of the middle, fourth and fifth finger of the throwing hand on the 2nd-4th laces from the tip of the ball nearest the index finger. Place the index finger on the seam that splits the laces. For younger players with smaller hands, you may choose to place the finger tips on the laces, instead of the finger joints.

Passing, *continued*

- Wrap the thumb around the end panel with the thumb tip secured against the ball, and the heel of the palm against the side panel. Ideally, there should be a slight air pocket between the palm and the ball, so as to allow the fingers and wrist to snap the ball into a spiral motion. The spiral motion is the key to velocity and trajectory.

- Obviously, the finger placement will vary with size of the hand.

Retreat:

- The ball is pulled into the belly at the snap.

- The throwing shoulder is turned by the open step, and becomes perpendicular to the line of scrimmage.

- The roll out, crossover, or back-pedal steps are executed.

- As the retreat is executed, the ball is pulled up to shoulder height, with both hands firmly cradling it.

- When the desired depth is reached, the QB plants his back foot to stop and shift his body momentum back towards the line of scrimmage. His non-throwing shoulder is perpendicular to the line of scrimmage, or towards his target. The ball is raised adjacent to the ear, and the front tip is cradled with non-throwing hand and held into position until ready to throw.

- In summary, it's a sequence of step, drop back, plant and throw.

Passing, *continued*

Throw:

🔑 Point the foot opposite the throwing arm, directly at target.

🔑 The ball is thrown from behind the shoulder and over the ear.

🔑 Extend the non-throwing arm out with fingers directly at target and palm to the ground. As the ball is thrown, step with the non-throwing foot. Bring the throwing hand forward, with the fingers rotating downward to create the spiral motion of the ball. For a short, straight and hard delivery, use a long step and release the ball at eye level. For longer deliveries, use a shorter step and release the ball at the crown of the helmet.

🔑 The throwing hand should be outstretched, with the palm facing down after the release.

 Pass Receivers

Passing is an integral part of the game and should be taught at all levels. However, the passing game is generally difficult in youth football. This is primarily due to the fact the experience level of the offensive unit typically isn't developed enough to provide the time a young quarterback needs to hit his receivers. That doesn't mean you should avoid it. In fact, I recommend at least 1-2 plays, regardless of the age level. The sooner they begin to learn it, the better prepared they will be for the next level.

I recommend you focus your teaching on catching techniques and learning / running basic traditional routes.

Running Back and Receiver Skills

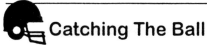 **Catching The Ball**

"Remember to emphasize look and tuck!"

- Always attempt to catch the ball with the hands, not the body. If the ball makes contact with the body first, it may bounce, particularly if it hits part of the shoulder/chest padding.

- Use the eyes to look the ball into the grasp of both hands. After the catch, immediately tuck the ball under one carrying arm, and prepare to run. Remember to emphasize **look and tuck**!

- As the ball approaches in flight, the eyes should be focused on the near tip until firmly grasped into the hands and tucked against the rib cage to begin the run. The eyes and head should follow the ball as it is tucked!

- If the pass is thrown at or above the chest height, bring the arms and hands up with the index fingers and thumbs coming together, and the palms facing the ball. It's like forming a hole for the ball to hit!

- If the pass is thrown below the chest, flip the wrists outward and down. This brings the "pinky" fingers together and spreads the thumbs. This forms more of a pocket for the ball to hit!

- For passes thrown over the shoulder, the hands go up with the "pinky" fingers together, and the palms facing back over the shoulder towards the ball.

- After the ball is caught and tucked, dip the up field shoulder and begin the run.

 **Stances**

- The stance for the tight end is usually a three point like the other linemen. The tight end obviously has to block and any other stance might signal the defenders a pass is planned.

- The stance for the wide receiver is different. He may elect to use the three point, but the rear foot is farther back for quicker acceleration. It is similar to a sprinter's stance.

- The wide receiver may also use an upright two point stance, with the torso forward, the arms and hands stretched slightly forward and just above the knees.

- The wide receiver must remember that he is a lineman, and must be properly positioned on the line of scrimmage.

Running Back and Receiver Skills

 ## Receiver Routes

The basic traditional routes are named and numbered. Moving from nearest the line of scrimmage to farther down the field, some common ones are: HOOK, IN, OUT, FLAG, FLY AND POST. An effective method for teaching them is to illustrate them in what is known as a ROUTE TREE. It's called that, because if you start at the base of the tree (line of scrimmage) and move up the trunk (downfield) you will see the routes branch off just like tree limbs. Numbers are required, because they are generally used in the designation of the play (covered more in Chapter 7).

I like to number them with odd for outside routes, and even for inside routes. Regardless of which side of the center you are on, if the number is even, your route is inside. Following is an illustration of the tree I prefer for youth level instruction.

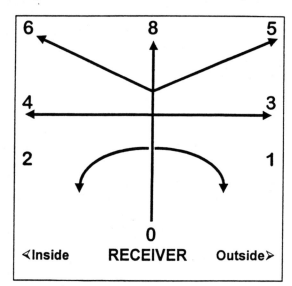

1. **Hook-Out**
2. **Hook-In**
3. **Square-Out**
4. **Square-In**
5. **Flag**
6. **Post**
8. **Fly**

 ## Running The Routes

In teaching the youth receiver, I recommend two fundamentals. First, teach the distance to be run by designating the number of steps for a given route before executing a cutting maneuver. Each step will move the receiver almost a yard. For example, a hook may be 3-5 steps off the line of scrimmage, while a flag may be 6-8 steps before the cut is made. Based on your age group, you can decide the number of steps for each route.

Second, teach the receiver to plant the foot opposite the direction he intends to go, and then cut quickly in the opposite direction. For example, on the 6 (post) plant the outside foot after about 6 steps, then cut back sharply with the inside foot toward the goal posts. Following are a few other tips that may be helpful in teaching your game.

Running Back and Receiver Skills

Running The Routes, *continued*

- Keep most of your pass routes ten yards or less.

- For each play, designate a primary and a secondary receiver on the same side of the field.

- If the primary is covered, go to the secondary receiver. If the secondary is covered, throw the ball beyond reach, or run like the dickens.

- Spend adequate time in practice developing the timing between the receivers and quarterback.

- Condition your offense to give the quarterback a good four seconds to execute the pass.

Learning The Hard Way: "The Case Of Too Many and Too Deep "

As I mentioned in an earlier chapter, my first few years were spent teaching 13 and 14 year old players. At that age, the passing game had real possibilities, and I intended to make the most of it. I used a drop-back passer, three receivers and tons of different routes, like the hitch-n-go, the z-out, and many more. I probably invented a new route about every three weeks. It was fun in practice, but man, did we suffer in the games!

My quarterback spent most of his time on his backside, because my routes were deep, and took several seconds to develop. The routes were so varied that the receivers were often confused, and the quarterback tried to scan the whole field, looking for an open man. If you could have looked down on my plays from the GOODYEAR blimp, it would probably have looked like an "Etch-A Sketch!"

A good friend of mine, who was a former receiver with the USC Trojans, gave me some advice. Guess what he told me? Reduce the routes to four or less! Designate a primary and secondary receiver! Don't throw the ball more that ten yards, unless you really have to! Get rid of the ball within 3-4 seconds! Make sure your receivers run disciplined routes!

As usual, my staff and I erased the drawing board and started over! Once again, the moral of the story always comes back to the point that you have to keep it basic with the younger ones, especially if our job is to prepare them for the next level!

Running Back and Receiver Skills

Summary

- Running backs and receivers can use a two or three point stance. Each has its advantages.

- The hand-off is critical, and the back should learn to accept it, not take it!

- The ball should be carried by placing the hand over the front end with the tip in between the index and middle finger. It should be held up against the rib cage.

- Just prior to contact, the free hand should be placed on top of the ball for protection.

- When running to the line of scrimmage, keep the knees slightly bent and torso forward. Kick the knees upward when moving through the neutral zone to avoid defenders wrapping their arms around the legs.

- Square the shoulders to the line of scrimmage when running straight ahead, or cutting back into the line from a lateral run.

- Use the side-step, stiff-arm and spin maneuver when evading a single defender.

- Develop a simple and rhythmic cadence for the snap count.

- The "clock technique" is an excellent instruction method for determining the initial step of the quarterback, or running back.

- Quarterbacks should learn the roll-out, crossover drop-back or back-pedal technique in setting up for the pass.

- Running backs on the toss, and receivers on the pass, should master the "look and tuck" technique before running.

- For receivers, if the pass is thrown at or above the chest height, bring the arms and hands up with the index fingers and thumbs coming together, and the palms facing the ball. It's like forming a hole for the ball to hit!

- If the pass is thrown below the chest, flip the wrists outward and down. This brings the "pinky" fingers together and spreads the thumbs. This forms more of a pocket for the ball to hit!

- Teach receivers to count the steps for a given route and use the plant foot before cutting to the direction.

- Keep the pass routes and the number of plays simple!

Fundamentals Of Kicking

 ## Youth Kicking Fundamentals

As in any level of football, teaching the kicking fundamentals requires both individual and team skills in the Punt, the Kick-off, the Extra Point - better referred to as the Point After Attempt (P.A.T.), and the Field Goal.

Any one of these dimensions of the game may become critical to a successful offensive attack. In reality, at the pre-junior high level, the P.A.T. and the Field Goal are often not utilized because of the skill level required to properly execute the fundamentals. That's not to say that they are not used rather, it is less common unless the team has some experienced coaches and/or exceptional players. Even if you have a talented kicker, success will depend on a sound deep snap and effective line blocking. Many games have been won or lost as a result of the kicking game, so don't overlook the importance of this dimension!

Finally, before you begin to teach, check your organization rules! Many youth recreation organizations recognize the skill level which is required for the kicking game and modify the rules accordingly, such as a free kick with no rushing, or merely advancing the ball a certain distance in lieu of a live kick. Such rules, if any, will certainly be relevant to how much time you spend on these fundamentals.

 ## Punting

Punting requires a skilled center-snapper and kicker. The snap of the ball must be into the thigh section of the punter at a distance of 8 - 10 yards, depending on the age and ability of the players. The starting center may not have the skills to execute a deep snap effectively, so find the most qualified player to perform this task. Obviously, you want to find the most qualified kicker as well, regardless of his normally assigned position. Following are the basic techniques for both the center and the kicker.

Center Stance and Snap:

- The feet are spread, with the toes aligned evenly toe to toe, and both hands are outstretched forward and on the football.

- The front hand grips front of the ball with the thumb on top of the ball; the index finger is wrapped down around the front strip; the other 2- 3 fingers are on the laces which are pointed toward the ground, and slightly to the sideline of the forward hand. This position helps the snapper execute a spiral motion as the ball is released to the kicker.

- The back hand is placed on the opposite side of the lower third of the ball, with the thumb on top.

- The ball should be targeted and snapped at the punters thigh pads.

Punting, *continued*

Punter Stance and Execution:

The punter has 4 basic techniques all of which are executed simultaneously:

1. Receiving the snap.

2. Rotating the laces, while taking the appropriate number of steps

3. Dropping the ball.

4. Swinging the kick foot into the ball

The ideal punt is designed with two steps, the kicking foot first, followed by the non-kicking foot, and swinging foot into the ball. The key in youth football is to get the kick executed, so use whatever method makes the kicker more successful. However, start by trying to teach the two step method.

Two Step Method:

- Proper stance is a very relaxed "breakdown" position with the torso bent slightly forward and the arms outstretched at a height above the ground, just about mid-section of the torso. Hands are positioned with the fingers pointed at the center, thumbs up toward the sky, and the open palms parallel to each other and spread about the width of the ball.

- The snap is looked into the hands. The same philosophy is taught to backs and receivers.

Punting, *continued*

Two Step Method, *continued*

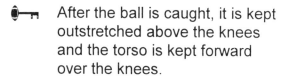 After the ball is caught, it is kept outstretched above the knees and the torso is kept forward over the knees.

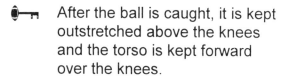 The first step is with the kick leg. As the step occurs, the ball is rotated to where the laces are upright and at a slight angle to the kick foot sidelines; front tip of the ball is turned slightly inward to allow more foot surface area to contact the ball and minimize the possibility of shanking the ball to the sidelines of the kicking foot.

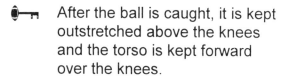 The second step is with the non-kicking leg.

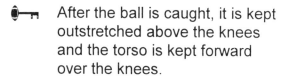 The ball is dropped as the foot swings forward at a point where the outside of the foot impacts the ball at the height of the non-kicking thigh. Dropping too high, or two low, will dramatically affect the trajectory of the kick. The leg is straightened forward with the knee locked and the top of the foot pointed and outstretched like a ballerina dancer.

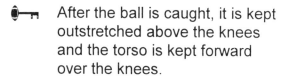 Keep the head down until the ball is kicked!

 ## The Extra Point (P.A.T.)

The P.A.T. requires three key players in the execution: the center, a holder, and the kicker. The fundamentals that should be taught are snapping the ball approximately two feet off the ground; receiving the ball and positioning it on the ground with laces toward the goal posts; a straight ahead approach by the kicker.

As in the punt, this play should be executed within two seconds in order to avoid the kick being blocked. Let's look at the fundamentals for each of the three players and how they work together.

The Center:

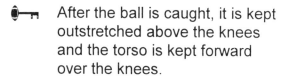 Stance and snap techniques are essentially the same as in the execution of the punt.

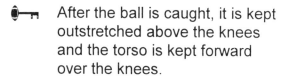 Key difference is the distance and the trajectory of the snap.

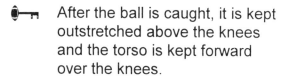 Ball will be snapped approximately 8 yards, at a height of two feet off the ground.

Fundamentals Of Kicking

The Holder:

- The receiver/holder is at a distance of approximately eight yards from the line of scrimmage.

- Right knee is on the ground and pointed toward the left sideline.

- Left knee is upright and positioned about six inches in front of the torso, also toward the left sideline.

- Torso is bent slightly forward and rotated to the center's backside.

- Arms and hands are outstretched toward the center and positioned like the running back receiving a toss.

- As ball is received, holder rotates the ball perpendicular to the ground with laces to the goal line.

- Ball is placed onto the ground or tee with the right hand index finger on the upper tip of the ball to hold in place until the ball is kicked.

- Left arm is withdrawn back to the outside of the left knee.

The Kicker :

- Kicker is approximately one and a half to two yards deep and directly behind the ball, this depends on age and ability.

- Body is positioned like the punter stance.

- As ball is snapped, kicker executes a two step approach:

1. First step is with the kicking foot. Distance of the step will have to depend on the kicker's ability; if the kick is getting executed too slowly, the step will have to be shortened to increase speed.

2. Second step is with the non-kicking foot. As the foot plants, the toes should land just behind and outside of the ball. Kicking foot swings through the ball with the toes hitting the ball just below the midpoint; as the ball makes contact the ankle is locked to keep the toes of the foot moving straight up to the sky, with heel pointed to the ground.

Fundamentals Of Kicking

The Kick-off

I recommend using the straight-ahead approach, although if the talent is available many coaches prefer using the soccer-style kick. The soccer-style kick can offer a lot of advantages in controlling hang time, distance, direction, etc. However, it also requires greater coaching expertise that may not be available in the younger age group organizations.

For that reason, I recommend sticking to the basic straight-ahead techniques as follows:

Straight Ahead Technique:

- Ball is placed upright on the kicking tee with the upper tip angled slightly back toward the kicker; laces are pointed toward the receiving team.

- Kicker positions approximately four to six yards directly behind the ball.

- As the kicker approaches the ball, the eyes are kept on the kick spot, which is just below the ball's midpoint.

- The torso is bent slightly forward throughout the approach and the kick.

- Kicking foot swings through the ball with the toes hitting the ball just below the midpoint. As the ball makes contact, the ankle is locked to keep the toes of the foot moving straight up to the sky, with heel pointed to the ground.

The Punt Formation

I recommend using one of two basic punt formations for youth league play:

1. The Tight Punt,

   or

2. The Spread Punt.

The Punt Formation, *continued*

Both formations require some basic fundamentals:

- Utilize your bigger players next to the center.

- Players on the line of scrimmage should be foot - to - foot.

- Use the following offensive line <u>basic</u> <u>blocking</u> <u>rules</u>. Block the defender in the inside gap first. If no one is in the inside gap, block the defender head up. If no defender is in the inside gap or head up, block the nearest linebacker inside or head up.

- Players should release and rush down field after hearing the "thud" of the ball leaving the punter's foot.

- *TIP! If punts are typically <u>short</u>, use a limited number of players to set up the return.*

1. **The Tight Punt Formation.** Two wingbacks are positioned in tight formation off the line of scrimmage, and six inches out from the tight end. A single blocking back is approximately three yards deep and positioned to the right of the center.

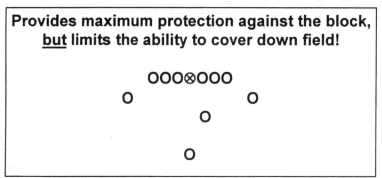

Provides maximum protection against the block, <u>but</u> limits the ability to cover down field!

2. **The Spread Punt Formation.** The tight ends are positioned three to four yards out from the offensive tackles. Two wingbacks are positioned in tight formation off the line of scrimmage, and six inches out from the tackles. A single blocking back is approximately three yards deep, and positioned to the right of the center.

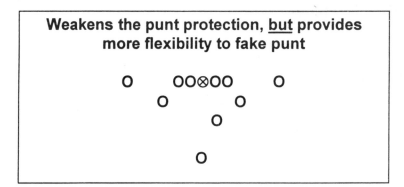

Weakens the punt protection, <u>but</u> provides more flexibility to fake punt

Fundamentals Of Kicking

The Punt Return

As with other aspects of this manual, I recommend keeping it simple. I recommend using a basic punt return formation and teaching return right or left. Check your league rules to determine any restrictions that may apply to rushing the kick. Some leagues attempt to help teams execute the kick by limiting the defensive lineup, i.e. no nose guard, free kick for certain ages, etc. If there are limitations, you will obviously want to concentrate on returning the punt vs. blocking.

Return Right Or Left: Illustrated from a 6-2 alignment

- Keep your ends and linebackers prepared for the fake punt.

- Assign numbers or positions to be used in forming a return wall.

- The defensive linemen should make contact with the offensive linemen's play side shoulder. If a right return is planned, they hit the left or outside shoulder to turn the offensive blocker away from the play with the initial hit.

- The defensive linemen retreat to their position on the wall.

Return Right

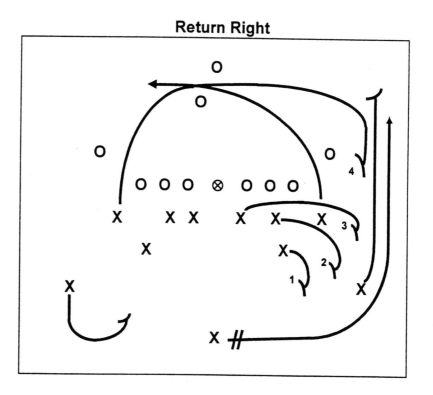

Fundamentals Of Kicking

The Kick-off Formation

I recommend teaching a traditional formation with five players on either side of the kicker, spread equally apart across the entire width of the field. The objectives are threefold:

1. Assign individual lanes of coverage.

2. Stay in the lane until the receiver has committed to a running direction.

3. Keep one player, often the kicker, back and in a safety type position, in case the coverage fails and the ball carrier breaks free.

- Players should line up anywhere from their thirty-five to thirty-eight yard line.

- Stance is upright, with hands on knees, or "breakdown," and facing into the middle of the field in order to see the kicker move past them and through the ball.

- Players begin their attack **after** the kicker has crossed their position and *begun the leg motion into the ball.*

- Ends on both sides of the field should remain in the outside lane until they reach the depth of the ball carrier; this guards against reverses and cutbacks.

ENDS-RULE OF THUMB-"Always make the tackle from the outside to inside!"

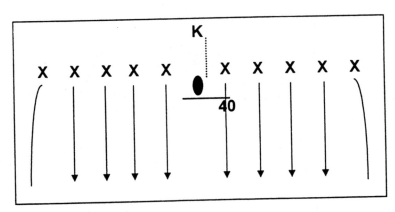

The Kick-off Return

As with the kick-off, I advocate K.I.S. (Keep It Simple) in developing your return game. I recommend using a traditional five man front wall. This allows sufficient protection against the on-side kick, and allows quick hits against many of the onrushing attackers. Back the front up with three short receivers, and three deep receivers. The objective is to provide maximum reaction time in getting to the kick,

The Kick-off Return, *continued*

regardless of what part of the field it reaches. Finally, use a simple numbering system for blocking assignments. Begin by numbering the kicking team 1 to 5 from outside to inside on both sides of the ball. Assign one of the numbers to your blockers, and generally plan on returning "up the middle."

- Stance for front five is a "breakdown," facing straight forward, with emphasis on watching for the on-side kick.

- Front five alignment is between the forty-five and fifty yard line. Remember, when the kick crosses the fifty yard line, it becomes a free ball. Your front five must be in a position to fall on it.

- Once the kick passes, all the front five players begin to set up for the retreat to their numbered blocking assignments.

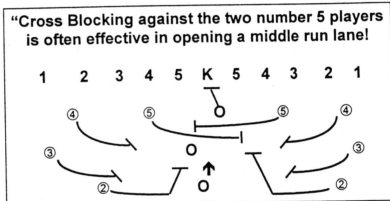

"Cross Blocking against the two number 5 players is often effective in opening a middle run lane!

Summary

- Select both the center and kicker on their ability to execute the techniques, regardless of which position they are normally assigned.

- Check your league rules regarding restrictions, or modifications, to the kicking game.

- The center snap is usually executed with two hands, and the ball is thrown to the punter, at height approximate to the kicker's thighs.

- The punter should use a two-step method.

- Dropping the ball two high or low can significantly impact the distance and trajectory of the ball.

- The center snap for a Point After Attempt requires a lower trajectory than the snap for the punt.

Summary, *continued*

- I recommend the straight-ahead approach for both the Point After Attempt and the Kick-off. As players progress to higher levels, soccer style kicking becomes fairly common and effective.

- The punt formation can be "Tight," to provide maximum protection for the kicker, or "Spread," to allow fake punts and better down-field coverage after the punt.

- Punt returns can be effective by forming an outside wall of blockers. They will block from the outside in, and form an outside lane for the ball returnee. Setting up the formation is more difficult when the kicks are typically short, so you may have to reduce the number of players in the wall.

- The kick-off formation should focus on designated lanes of coverage, outside protection against cutbacks and reverses, and a safety position for breakdowns in coverage.

- On kick-off returns establish a 5-3-3 alignment and set up the return blocking assignments by assigning numbers to the kick return team.

- Unless the league rules limit the game, all aspects should be practiced weekly. If you are unprepared, the consequences can range from penalties, offensive returns for touchdowns, confusion, fumbles, etc. ***Your team cannot afford to overlook this dimension of the game!***

Defensive Fundamentals

 ## Keys To Defensive Fundamentals

Teaching youth defense should focus on the following skills: stopping the offensive initial charge; shedding the opponent; spotting the ball carrier; pursuing the ball carrier; defending the forward pass; and above all, using the proper form in tackling the ball carrier. These basic skills should be taught using a limited number of defensive formations. The primary emphasis is usually placed on stopping the run. Pass defense is important and should be taught, but allocate the time spent on practicing it relative to the age group and the competition's ability to throw.

I like to teach a THREE step basic approach and then select two or three traditional defensive formations, which were designed to stop the running attack. Defensive alignments will be discussed and illustrated in a later chapter.

 ## Fundamentals Of Tackling

In my opinion, this is a critical technique which should be taught by the book and practiced daily! Proper tackling form requires the use of the entire body. Particular emphasis must be placed on placement of the head during the tackle!

Players are not allowed to use the helmet to Butt, or Ram into the body of an opponent. In addition, they are not allowed to Face Tackle or Spear. These rules were established some time ago by the National Federation Of State High School Associations to reduce the risk of injury to the head and neck. The key here is hitting the body of the opponent. As you will see below, it's okay to drive the facemask through the ball when it's off to the side in a normal carrying position. The shoulder is used to hit the body! **Remember - Teach Them To Keep "Heads Up." Preach It! Enforce It!**

 ## Direct Head On Tackle

The player should assume the "Breakdown," or "Ready" position, with the feet spread shoulder width and in a toe-to-instep alignment. The knees should be slightly bent and the forearms raised to a parallel position to the ground, with fists doubled and pointed straight ahead. The head is up and the back is straight.

This position puts the player in a position to move, hit, or counter a hit. If the technique is wrong, the player will be off balance, increasing the risk of being knocked to the ground.

Direct Head On Tackle, *continued*

🗝 The tackler should move directly at the ball carrier, keeping the eyes on the player's midsection.

🗝 Drop the shoulders and dip the hips just before contact, and drive one shoulder up and into the mid-section of the ball carrier, using the force from the lower body.

🗝 As contact occurs, drive the facemask to the outside of the ball carrier's upper body and into the football. Keep the eyes open and the head up at all times.

🗝 Swing the arms outward and parallel to the ground. As the shoulder makes contact, wrap the arms around the ball carrier and into the lower center of the back.

🗝 Pull and squeeze, while using the power of the legs to lift up and drive through the opponents upper body.

Angle Tackle

🗝 Players should assume the "break-down" position.

🗝 The tackler runs at an angle which will intercept the ball carrier's path.

🗝 In the approach to the runner, point the face mask at the runner's inside foot as a way to position the body for a possible evasive cut back, side-step or cross-over step by the runner.

🗝 Drop the shoulders and dip the hips just before contact, and drive the shoulder into the hip of the ball carrier. Drive the facemask across the front of the ball carrier's mid-section and to the outside arm. Remember, it's across the front of the mid-section.

Angle Tackle, *continued*

- Keep the eyes open and the head up at all times.

- Swing the arms outward and parallel to the ground; as the shoulder makes contact, wrap the arms around the ball carrier's waist. Pull and squeeze, while using the power of the legs to lift up and drive through the opponent's upper body.

- Keep the legs pumping and drive the ball carrier to the ground.

  Tip-Always position the head in front of the ball carrier. If the head goes behind the ball carrier, the runner can use a spin technique, which will likely throw the defender loose from the runner's body.

Three Step Approach To Defensive Play - (SSS)

1. **Stop the blocker.**

2. **Spot the ball.**

3. **Shed the blocker and pursue to the ball.**

Interior Linemen: Tackle To Tackle

There are numerous theories on how to play the defensive front line. Some coaches like to have their linemen control the offender and protect a hole. Others believe the guards should play control and the tackles and ends pursue the ball carrier, while some advocate assigning responsibility to a gap. In youth play, I recommend the control theory, with occasional gap attacks. Gap assignment is probably the easiest to teach. On the other hand, control theory can offer the young defender a broader base of skill development. Control can be taught by using a three step approach.

In addition, the entire defense should learn pursuit. Each player should be taught to pursue to a point on the field which will allow them to intercept a ball carrier's path when the runner has gone laterally to the sidelines, or broken upfield across the neutral zone. Defenders should learn they should never attempt to catch a runner by trailing him, if they can use an angle first.

Effective defensive line play begins with the stance, and reacting on the snap of the ball.

Defensive Fundamentals

Interior Linemen: Tackle To Tackle, *continued*

 The stance is either three or four point, depending on the player's ability. The four point typically enables a quicker and harder hit into the opponent.

Tip- more weight can be placed on the front hand(s), since the first move is to stop the blocker!

 Depending on whether you use control or gaps, the stance alignment should be helmet to helmet, or helmet to inside shoulder, or helmet to outside shoulder for small offensive line gaps, one to two feet. The youth organization rules may require the defensive player to align head-up on the opponent regardless of the offensive formation used, **<u>so check your rules</u>**.

Three Step Approach As Ball Is Snapped

1. **Stop** the initial charge first. Lock the eyes onto the offensive center's hands, or the ball and fire out into the blocker on the first movement of the ball. Hit the blocker underneath the upper body to stand him upright. Remember, the blocker is going to try the same technique on the defender!

2. **Spot** the runner with the ball after stopping the initial charge. As contact is made with the blocker, get the head up and to one side, so that the runner can be seen. One technique some coaches teach is to slide the head into the V of the blocker's neck on either side as contact is made.

3. **Shed** the blocker with one of four basic techniques, and get ready to make the tackle or pursue the ball carrier.

Hand Or Forearm Shiver Control Technique

If you are going to teach the Control technique, I recommend the following instructions. Fire out of the stance into the upper body of the blocker and slam the open palms **or** forearms/palms down into the opponent's chest pads to upright him and take away his forward momentum. Push against the direction of his resistance with the hips and legs, and pull/push the blocker laterally to the outside or inside gap. Don't allow the blocker's body to go down and to either side of the legs. If the blocker gets that position, the defender may be pushed

Defensive Fundamentals

Hand Or Forearm Shiver Control Technique, *continued*

down the line of scrimmage and away from the play. Make the slam to the blocker's chest before he gets into position to make the block. **Keep the body in a position to move laterally to either side of the blocker's head. Never try to go around the blocker's backside to get to the runner. This is the key to playing Control Defense!**

 ### Forearm-Block For Gap Attack

Swing the forearm opposite to the gap to be protected into the opponent's "V" of the neck between helmet and shoulder pad. The fist is pointed upward and the opposite hand is used to push the blocker laterally to the side. For example, if the defender is attacking his right gap, he will use his left forearm to stop the blocker's initial charge, and slide into the gap looking for the runner.

 ### Arm Rip For Gap Attack   DG/DT

Swing the forearm opposite to the gap to be protected up and underneath the gap arm of the blocker, and use the opposite hand to push forward and through into the backfield. This technique is used primarily for quick penetration and/or pass rushing.

 ### Arm Swim For Gap Attack   DE

Step with the gap side foot and slam the gap side hand into the blocker's bicep or shoulder pad, to push him up and away from the gap. Throw the opposite arm up and over the blocker's helmet in a swim-like motion. This technique should allow the defender to slide off the blocker's side and into the gap.

Finish Off The 3 Steps

Regardless of which technique is used, Control or Gap attack, after stopping the initial charge, spotting the runner, and shedding the blocker, either move into the open gap to meet the runner, or pursue to the ball. If the runner is within one or two inside or outside gaps, move laterally down the line of scrimmage. If the runner is beyond that area, turn and pursue to a spot up-field which will allow intercepting the ball carrier's path. This is what makes defenses great! Don't stop until the whistle blows!

 ## A Word About "Keys" and "Reads"

The terms "Keys" and "Reads" are commonly used for defensive play. Although some coaches use the terms interchangeably, others use them for separate meanings. However, both are techniques which are used to teach a defender to react to an offensive player's initial movement at the snap of the ball. For example, you might instruct the linebacker to key on an offensive guard. If the guard's first movement is forward and across the neutral zone, the linebacker knows it is a running play. However, if the first movement is a setup to pass-block, the linebacker will know pass and may have to retreat into a zone coverage.

The term Read is often used to teach defenders to key on more than one player. Using the linebacker example, he may be instructed to look beyond the lineman into the backfield, and key on two running backs. For example, he may be taught to read and react if the backs criss-cross, or sweep to a particular side, etc. Reads are typically developed as a result of scouting the opponent and identifying consistent offensive movements on certain plays. Keys on the other hand, are usually rules of thumb on how to react on any offensive play.

 ## A Word About Stunts

A defensive "stunt" is a technique in which one or more defensive players, usually two, execute a combined movement to fool the offensive blockers. The objective is to allow a player to penetrate, or "blitz," into the backfield in hopes of stopping the offensive play for a loss. An effective stunt is one designed to stop an expected offensive play.

One of the more common examples is to have the down defensive lineman charge into a designated gap, hoping the blocker will follow him. As the blocker follows, a stacked linebacker will attempt to shoot into the backfield through the opening vacated by the blocker who followed the down lineman. Another example, such as in the "6-2", is to have the defensive guards shoot into the "A" gap, the defensive tackles into the "C" gap, hopefully leaving the "B" gap open for the linebackers to penetrate into the backfield with ease.

Defensive stunts require an objective, practice and clear signals as to when the stunt is to be executed. Inside linebackers usually get the signal from the sidelines and have the responsibility to communicate to the other members of the unit prior to the offensive snap.

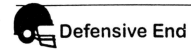
Defensive End

The defensive end's key responsibilities are to block down on the offensive tight end, to stop the run-off tackle, pursue laterally and turn the sweep run to the inside, rush the passer, and protect against the reverse. Obviously, it's one of the most critical defensive positions on the team. In fact, for the younger age groups, I recommend putting two of your top five players at this position, even the quarterback!

- The defensive end should be aligned on the outside shoulder of the offensive tight end. If there is a flanker adjacent to the tight end, you <u>may</u> want to consider aligning the defensive end in between them, and down in a three-point stance. This will help him split the double-team block.

- If aligned in an upright position, the stance should be a break-down position, with the outside foot dropped back with a toe to heel or instep alignment. This provides stability against the kick-out block by the offensive end, and permits a quick lateral step to the outside to pursue the run sweep, or rush the passer.

- The defensive end should key on the offensive tight end's head, or down hand. If there is no tight end, he can either key on the nearside back, or the center. As movement occurs, stop the blocker by thrusting the inside forearm up and into the offensive end's sternum, on the outside jersey number. This is followed by bringing the outside hand's open palm laterally into the offensive end's outside shoulder pad, and shoving him to the inside, hand shiver technique.

- Keep the back straight and use the legs to drive through the blocker.

- Keep the head and eyes up, and spot the ball. Keep an awareness that blockers may be pulling laterally from the interior line of scrimmage to lead the play, and/or from the backfield. The break-down position is critical to fight off such blocks.

- Pursue to the ball.

Off Tackle Run:

- Stop the offensive end's charge.

- Spot the ball.

- Shed the block and move across the blocker's facemask and into the hole making a head up or angle tackle on the ball carrier.

Defensive End, *continued*

Other Interior Line Run:

- Stop the offensive end's charge.

- Spot the ball.

- Move across the blocker's facemask. When the ball crosses the neutral zone, turn and run at an angle back, across and into open field to intercept ball carrier's path.

- Use hand shivers to keep other blockers off the lower body.

Run Sweep to Defender's Side:

- Stop the offensive end; spot the ball; shed the offensive end and other blockers. Keep the knees bent and the feet spread for balance in fighting off lead blockers.

- Move laterally to the side, using crossover steps and keep the shoulders square to the line of scrimmage; keep an "inside eye to inside eye" alignment with the runner while running to the sideline.

- The primary responsibility is to force the runner to turn up and inside of the defensive end before reaching the sideline.

Run Sweep Away From The Defender's Side:

- Stop the offensive end's charge.

- Spot the ball.

- There are two different techniques commonly used:

  A. Stay at the end position until the ball carrier crosses the neutral zone on the far side of the field; don't pursue the ball until certain the play is not a reverse. Turn and pursue to the ball by running at an angle toward the far side corner of the end zone, running directly at the upright orange pylon will provide the correct angle. This is often referred to as the "Hero Play."

  or

  B. Pursue into the backfield to a depth of the deepest back and trail the play at that depth. If the play does reverse back, the defensive end should be positioned to force the runner back into the interior of the line for additional defensive support.

Linebacker

The linebacker's key responsibilities are to stop the inside and off tackle run; pursue to the outside and assist with stopping the outside sweep run; defend against the pass by guarding a specific offensive player, or guarding a zone within the secondary.

Many coaches will utilize their most talented defenders at this position, since the job requires so many responsibilities. The position requires quickness, aggressiveness, understanding of the game, and the desire to tackle at full speed. At one time or another, most coaches will get an opportunity to coach a player who just seems to have an extra sense of where the ball is going to be. When that happens, put him at linebacker!

- The stance is an upright two point in a break-down position.

- The toes of the outside foot are aligned with the instep of the inside foot.

- Inside linebackers are generally taught to key on the nearest interior lineman's down hand or movement of the head. They can also learn to key on the near side running back. I personally prefer teaching to key on the quarterback. In the youth ages, the quarterback is usually consistent on how he opens with the first step, and this can help the linebacker quickly determine the direction of the play.

- If the blocker charges straight ahead, the linebacker steps into the blocker, and stops the charge with a hand shiver, or forearm thrusts.

Defensing The Offensive Blocker:

- Linebacker spots the ball, sheds the blocker, and pursues to the ball carrier.

- If a blocker pulls down the line of scrimmage, the playside linebacker follows him by moving laterally down the defensive side of the line.

- Linebacker spots the ball, and pursues to the point of the runner's attack.

- He must shed blocker(s) and get to the ball carrier.

- If the blocker moves into pass protection block, the linebacker retreats to pass defend a designated protection zone, usually a hook back and outside approximately five yards from the line of scrimmage, unless he has instructions to blitz.

- In pass protection coverage, he looks for receivers coming into the zone, and defends the pass.

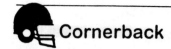

Cornerback

Cornerback has the responsibility to stop the outside run, defend against short and deep passes, and pursue inside to assist with a run through the neutral zone. The position requires quickness, speed, open field tackling, and the ability to move in any direction.

- Stance is similar, yet slightly different, than the breakdown position. Defensive backs have to be able to accelerate forward or backward quickly. An effective stance has the outside foot back with the toes even with the heel of the up foot. The feet are closer together than the shoulder width alignment of other stances, in order to back pedal or move forward more quickly with the first step. The front foot is used as a plant foot in pushing off for the back pedal, or moving forward to stop the run. The knees are slightly bent; the arms are bent at the elbow, and the hands held just outside of the thighs.

- For a standard tight offensive formation, the position lines up approximately five yards off the line of scrimmage, and approximately two-three yards outside the defensive end. Against a spread offense, alignment will generally be just inside the widest split player.

- First responsibility is to stop the pass; secondary responsibility is to stop the run.

  Tip: with the youngest player age groups, there is usually limited passing, and the first responsibility is to stop the outside run! Generally, ages nine and above should learn to defend the pass first!

Pass Responsibility:

- Key is to look through the offensive line and watch the movement of the quarterback, while staying aware of the near side offensive end or flanker.

- Move as the quarterback moves; if QB signals pass, retreat with the back pedal and defend a predetermined short or deep zone, or designated man.

- If a receiver routes down the sideline, the cornerback should attempt to run inside the receiver, and force the player to the sideline. This takes away some the receiver's space to catch the pass.

- Run step for step with the receiver, while keeping between him and the goal line.

- Watch the receiver's eyes, which will typically signal when the pass is coming his way.

- Extend both arms and play to intercept the pass.

Cornerback, *continued*

Run Responsibility:

- Once the cornerback determines run to the near side, he steps forward and comes up fast, ready to pursue an angle to the outside, if the back sweeps.

- The responsibility is to tackle the runner, or force the play inside, where the linebacker should be in a position to make the tackle.

- In approaching the runner, keep the face mask targeted at the inside leg of the runner. This helps to make an inward move, if the runner attempts to evade with a side-step, or cross-over step to the inside.

- If the runner is led by a blocker, the corner must target the blocker's outside jersey number. The blocker should be stopped with a shoulder-block, or forearm thrust on the outside number. The outside hand's open palm can be used to shove the blocker to the inside path of the runner, if a cut is made. If the runner does not cut inward, the corner continues driving through to the outside, and pursues the ball.

 Safety

The physical requirements and fundamental techniques are the same for both the corner and safety positions. A key difference is that the safety has responsibility for the deeper pass routes. However, some coaches now use the safety to play the short underneath zones and run protection, while forcing the cornerbacks to play the deep routes. The player in the traditional deep role has to ensure that the receiver does not get behind him on a pass route. At the same time, he has to be able to reverse direction and provide run support if the pass is a decoy, and the running back breaks into the secondary.

Different defensive formations will call for different alignments and responsibilities for the position. Some defenses use a single deep safety aligned over the center approximately eight yards from the line of scrimmage. The younger youth teams will often use this formation to allow an additional linebacker, or linemen, to stop the running game. Other formations may use two deep safeties aligned over the defensive tackle, but six to eight yards off the line of scrimmage. Finally, two safeties may be used with one designated as "strong" and the other as "free." The strong safety allows placement of one the safeties on the strong side of the offensive formation to stop the short pass, and/or running attack. The free safety normally has pass defense responsibility.

Defensive Fundamentals

Safety, *continued*

Pass Responsibility:

- Spot the alignment of the offensive ends and flankers. Think pass!

- Keep the eyes on the quarterback, and if a pass play develops, begin looking for the receiver and back pedal at an angle to intercept the receiver's path.

- If the receivers release down field, pass-protect in the designated zone or man-to-man, as determined by the coach's defensive strategy.

- If the run develops into the interior of the line, run to the point of attack.

- If the run develops laterally, run east/west until ball crosses neutral zone, and pursue an angle to the running back's inside leg.

- Stop any open field blockers with hand-shiver or shoulder-block on the outside shoulder of the blocker, and pursue to the ball across the face mask of the blocker. Never run around a lead blocker.

- Give backward ground, if necessary, to get across the front of the blocker and get a position that will allow a sufficient angle to the runner's path.

 A Word About Zone Coverage

Defensive pass coverage usually consists of protecting *zones,* or designating a specific position, "man," to guard, regardless of the zone. My preference is to teach zone coverage, because it can be easily remembered, and is generally effective for youth league ball.

Zones are simply areas of the field a defender must protect. A four or three zone can be established by dividing the width of the field into three or four equal areas, running vertically from the line of scrimmage to the defender's goal line. These may also be referred to as "lanes." Zones can also be designated to protect against the shorter type passes, like the "hook" and "square-in." These are typically the responsibility of the linebacker. To keep it simple (KIS), I teach a rotating coverage technique.

I teach a three or four deep zone, depending on the play, and whether one or two safeties are used. If there are two safeties, a four deep zone would be used to defend pass plays, and a three deep would be used to defend against the sweeps.

1. If the play was an obvious pass, the corners would have deep coverage on the outside zones, and the safeties would have the same for their inside zones. In other words, you have four deep lanes stretching all the way to the goal line, each covered by a defender. The linebackers are instructed to hook back and out, to provide coverage for two short and underneath zones.

A Word About Zone Coverage, *continued*

2. If the play is a sweep, the cornerbacks and safeties will have to rotate toward the flow of the ball. The reason is that the playside cornerback will need to come up to help defend against the run. When this happens, his deep zone responsibility will have to be handled by the playside safety, who rotates over. The playside safety will be replaced by the backside safety, who will be replaced by the backside cornerback. The coverage has now turned into a three deep zone. This is illustrated below. Notice the linebackers protecting the short zones.

Example: 3 Deep Rotation Against Sweep Action

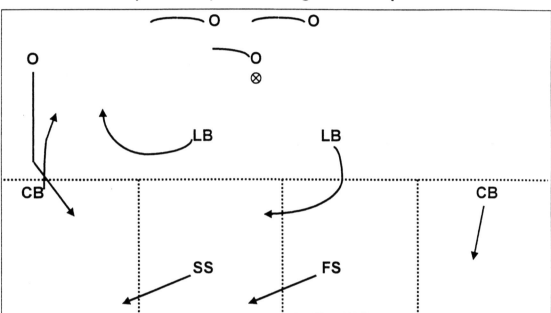

Learning The Hard Way: "The Dreaded Yellow Flag"

It was late in the game and we were behind. Momentum had swung our way and you could just feel the kids' desire to win. If we stopped their offense on the current possession, we would benefit from good field position, and have a good chance of gaining the lead.

On third down and long, the offense ran a sweep play towards our sidelines. Our defense swarmed the runner and tackled him for a loss, directly in front of where I was standing. As I began to jump for joy, I noticed the official reaching for his back pocket. Out came the flag, and he tossed it into the air. We all seemed to stand motionless, waiting for his call. He called for the offensive team captain, and we knew it was against us. The call was personal foul for a late hit, technically known as illegal personal contact. The penalty was 15 yards and a first down.

I had observed the player who had allegedly committed the foul, and I was convinced the official made a bad call. I became angry and began to shout and scream. The official gave me his explanation, and cautioned me to step back and

Learning The Hard Way: "The Dreaded Yellow Flag," *continued*

off of the field. I wasn't satisfied and continued to scream at him. Then it happened, another yellow flag. This time it was on me, for unsportsman-like conduct. Another 15 yards were assessed against my defense.

Any chance we had to win suddenly vanished. In retrospect, I acted inappropriately, regardless of whom was right or wrong. My behavior had several impacts: it put our defense in a no-win situation, it caused me great embarrassment, and I set a poor example for the players and spectators. Don't get me wrong, it's okay to disagree with an official's calls, but there is a procedure expected to be followed. Besides, how many times have you seen them change their call? The more important thing is the example we set for our kids!

Summary

- Use a three step approach to defensive line play. <u>Stop</u> the initial charge, <u>Spot</u> the ball, and <u>Shed</u> the blocker.

- Never allow tackling with the top of the helmet or facemask. It's against high school and college rules, because it can cause serious injury!

- Always tackle from the breakdown position, using the shoulder, hips, feet spread, back arched and head up.

- Use the eyes to focus on the mid-section, drive the facemask through the ball, with head up.

- Wrap the arms around the defender; use the legs and hips to lift and drive him to the ground.

- Teach both the head-on technique and the angle technique; most tackles actually occur at an angle.

- Several techniques are available for defensive linemen, including the forearm-block and hand-shiver which are used to stop the initial block.

- The *arm rip* and *arm swim* are effective for pass rushing; choose the one that fits the players physical abilities.

- The interior defensive linemen can be taught cover or gap responsibility.

- Each defensive position should be taught to "key" on an offensive player prior to the snap. Some positions, like the linebacker, may "read" two players prior to the snap, rather than keying on just one.

- Defensive pass protection is through the use of "Zone" or "Man" coverage strategies.

Offensive Formations and Strategies

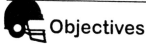

Objectives

There are several objectives in this chapter:

1. Explain how to develop an offensive formation and designate plays.
2. Offer my alternatives to the traditional methods of offensive instruction.
3. Illustrate different types of offensive formations.

For your information, the game has been around since the turn of this century. The first offensive formations were the single wing, and other variations which required the center to deep snap to a back for a running play. Today there are probably no less than 20 basic formations, with literally hundreds of variations, including running, and particularly passing. It absolutely amazes me how college and pro receivers can remember all those complicated sets. As exciting as that may seem, it often tempts inexperienced youth coaches to implement a formation which is too complicated for the age group, and/or a bad fit for the level of the team's talent.

I'm going to offer you some of my simplified teaching methods, and suggest some approaches on how to select your offensive strategy. Finally, we will take a peek at just some of many different offensive formations of today's game, simply to illustrate the variability involved.

Formation Rules

Before we get into explaining teaching methods, there are a couple of basic rules, which must be followed for your offensive formation:

1. Seven players are required to be on the line of scrimmage prior to the offensive snap of the ball. The linemen typically align next to each other with two - three foot splits between them. One, or both, offensive ends may split away from the tackle and towards the sideline, provided they are still aligned on the line of scrimmage.

2. The offensive center is the only player who may cross into the "neutral zone" so he may place his hands on the ball in order to snap it to the quarterback. The "Neutral" zone can be defined as the length of the ball from tip to tip, when placed down ready for snap. This distance separates the offense and defense, so that neither can cross their tip end of the ball prior to its being snapped.

3. The offensive backs cannot line up on the line of scrimmage, or the seven man rule will be violated.

If the guard, tackle or end have any part of their bodies across their tip end of the ball, it is considered a rule violation, and a penalty is enforced. In addition, if they are lined up too far from the neutral zone, they will be considered aligned in the backfield and thus, the seven man rule is violated; also a penalty ensues.

Offensive Formations and Strategies

Formation Rules, *continued*

Therefore, you must teach them to get proper alignment by positioning the tip of the helmet through an imaginary line, drawn parallel to the line of scrimmage, and through the waist of the snapper.

A couple of practical tips include using a nylon string to stretch through the waist of the center towards the sideline. Have each player practice this alignment with and without the string. Another method is to have the guard, tackle, and end stretch their arms out to the side, and place their hands on the adjacent players' shoulder pads. Caution! Some players will be shorter or taller relative to the other players, and will have to adjust their alignment to compensate.

Traditional Play Designations

The naming, or designation, of an offensive play can range from simple to complex. Fortunately, there is an age-old standard that should be used in teaching. The traditional system for teaching and executing an offensive play is to use a **formation name**, a type of **play name**, and **numbering** for running and passing plays.

Formation Name is simple enough and straightforward. For example, Wing-T, Right or Left, I-Formation Right or Left, etc. This designates how the running backs will align prior to execution of the play.

Numerics is the traditional method for designating which running back will receive the hand-off, and the point of attack along the offensive line of scrimmage. Following the formation name, two numbers are used to designate who gets the ball, and where it is going. The first of the two numbers designates the running back who will get the ball, as illustrated in the T-formation below:

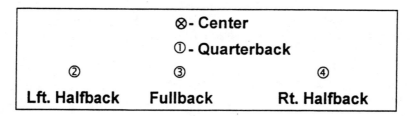

Numbers along the offensive line of scrimmage designate the "hole," or point of attack, through which the running back will attempt to run. For example, the offensive line positions <u>or</u> the gaps in between them, (I prefer the gaps) are numbered to designate where the running back is to attack. On the right side of the center, the gaps, <u>or</u> the positions, may be designated with even numbers two to eight from the center towards the sideline. On the left side of center, the line positions, <u>or</u> the gaps, may be designated with odd numbers, one to seven towards the sideline.

Traditional Play Designations, *continued*

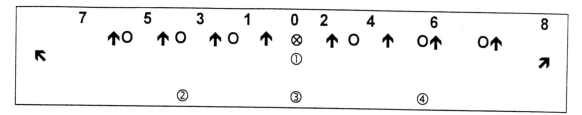

Play Names can be whatever you choose to designate. However, some names are commonly used throughout most coaching circles. Some examples are: "Quick," "Wham," "Power," "Sweep," "Bootleg," "Trap," and "Counter." This common usage obviously helps the player's learning ability as he progresses from level to level.

Thus, you have the **Formation Name**, a **Double Number** designating who gets the ball, where to attack and the **Play Name**. For example, T-46 Quick designates the formation is a Straight-T, with the right halfback (4) receiving the hand-off, and attacking (off tackle) the 6 gap in a straight ahead type of running play (Quick), with no other backs or linemen lead blocking. Notice the illustration below:

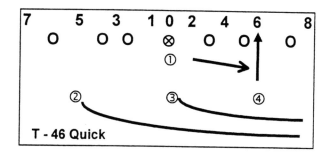

T - 46 Quick

Finally, the receivers and their pass routes, may be designated with a series of one to three numbers, indicating the type of route. The numbers called designate the pass routes (remember the "Pass Tree" in Chapter 4) for the receivers from left to right, respectively. For example, a Wing-T Right 653 Drop Back would designate the left tight end to the post (6), the right tight end to the flag (5) and the wingback to the sideline (3). This is just one of many methods, and, as you can imagine, they get more complex with age and skill. A simpler method is to just name the pass play and have the affected receivers remember what routes they must run. For example, "Sprint Out" right require the same routes, but, the name may make it easier to remember.

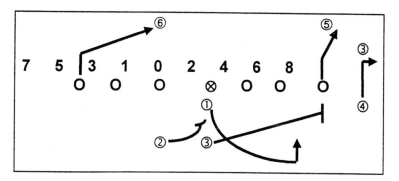

Offensive Formations and Strategies

Traditional Play Designations, *continued*

All the foregoing seems fairly simple, right? Try to teach this to an eight, nine or ten year old who is just beginning the game! Don't panic; it's not as difficult as it may seem, but it does require a good teacher and a systematic way of learning.

Again, the systems I have just described are traditional, but there are some alternative methods which may be more appropriate for your team, particularly for the running game.

Alternative Methods To Traditional Designation Systems

I'm not the first coach to arrive at this conclusion, by any means, but I did realize some time ago, that the numbering system is typically difficult for the younger player to learn. *It is important that they eventually learn it in order to advance to the junior and high school levels, but that can be accomplished in many ways, and at the right time. The more important consideration is to learn the execution of the basic physical techniques of the game, and the offensive and defensive play strategies.*

There are other techniques which may enhance the learning ability:

First, consider replacing the offensive formation with color codes. For example, a T-formation can be called Red; A Wing-T Right may be called Green; An I can be called Blue, etc. A Green Right would designate a Wing-T with the Wing Player on the right side of the line. Kids seem to recall color codes easily.

Second, replace the numbering system with the name of the play, and the side of the line to be attacked. For example, Power Right instead of 26 Power. Eliminating the numbers can make the play easier to remember for both the back and the linemen. In addition, it can provide more flexibility for the back to pick an opening other than the numbered hole.

Third, designate play names to certain backs only. For example, the tailback might be assigned Sweeps, Quicks, Powers, and Draws, while the fullback would be assigned Blasts and Bucks, and the wingback assigned counters and traps. It doesn't take long to remember which plays you are assigned to run.

Finally, don't take the **linemen** for granted. If they don't know the play blocking responsibilities, there's obviously a high probability the back won't be successful. One technique I've found successful is to assign <u>nicknames</u> to the linemen which relate to the name of the play. One to two lineman are the key blockers on any given running play, so I generally assign them nicknames for the plays for which they have responsibility. For example, if the play is a trap and the pulling guard is the key blocker, that player might have one of his nicknames as "Trapper John." He may also be a key blocker on the fullback blast, in which case he will have an additional nickname of "Buckeye Blaster." I know what you are thinking, sounds pretty corny, right? Maybe so, but it certainly enhances the learning curve, and the more creative you can be, the more fun the players experience.

Offensive Formations and Strategies

Traditional Play Designations, *continued*

One of the drills I utilize is to put the offensive line down on one knee, and when I call the nickname, the player to whom the nickname is assigned must quickly jump upright, signifying he knows it's his nickname. He is then required to tell where the play is going and his blocking responsibility. Doubt if you will, but I've had seven and eight year old players responding to this drill with perfection! The objective is to teach, and it works with <u>fun</u> included.

 ## Supplemental Methods to X's and O's

X's and O's is the age old foundation for illustrating plays. Why? Because it is a simple method to illustrate and can be used to adjust plays with the quickness of the pen, or marker. You can illustrate the play in the sand, on the back of a napkin, or any medium on which you can draw. It's a common language for coaches, players, and spectators of the game. However, with today's systems technology, reproduction, and the personal computer, there is another method that I've found to be extremely effective in teaching.

As a supplement to the X's and O's, graphic pictorials of the players are an excellent teaching tool. The reason is simple. It's easier to associate with a picture representation than abstract letters or symbols, such as X's and O's. You will get the idea when you review the Playbook section of this manual. I've taken the effort to illustrate formations and plays with pictures, in addition to the X's and O's. I've developed my playbook in that format, and even taken it a step further, by enlarging the pictures through reproduction graphics, cutting them out individually, attaching a small magnet and placing them on a magnetic bulletin board, which I use for instruction. During practice or games, I can hang the board on a nail, set it up on a tripod, or just prop it up, and I've got an instant classroom! You can move the figures at will to illustrate direction, where to make contact, and emphasize what needs to happen where and when, in the execution of the play. My players identify easily with their own position, the opponent to be blocked or defensed, and the development of the player interaction as the play develops. It seems to work especially well for the younger and inexperienced.

It may sound like a great deal of trouble and expense, but it really isn't. It's all a matter of how much time and preparation you are willing and able to put into your program. It's **also** about breaking paradigms, a preconceived notion that there's only one way to do something. This method may do nothing for you, and that's okay. However, it's proven to me that there may always be a better way to teach, and one of my personal goals is to keep an open mind to what works best. In fact, I'm willing to predict that in the not too distant future, we will be using computer lap tops and projection systems, or something comparable, to do the same thing. <u>Remember</u>, the idea is to teach and prepare them for the next level!

"Keep it Simple"

Offensive Formations and Strategies

 ## Developing Your Offensive Strategy

At this point, I would like to offer you some tips to develop your offensive strategy. Once again, I encourage you to use the "F.A.S.T." approach in all aspects of your game. Beyond that, however, you need to determine what type of offensive attack you will employ.

I recommend considering and selecting from several approaches, while testing against key criteria. Let's review how you might go about the task.

 ## Evaluating Skills and Abilities Approach

- Does your league have constraints on the types of defenses that may be utilized, or is it anything goes, for example, a ten man defensive line?

- What is the average experience level of your team? Are the players coming together for the first time, or have they moved up together from the lower level?

- Is the offensive line capable of executing pulling and trap techniques?

- What skill level will they have in pass blocking?

- Are the running backs blessed with quickness and speed, and is there at least one back who can perform lead blocking on power running, such as the bruiser fullback?

- Is your quarterback capable of executing the passing game, and does he have sufficient talent among the receivers?

- If your quarterback misses the big game for whatever reason, will your team be able to execute the same set of plays?

- Does your team have a sufficient number of coaches?

 ## Play Selection Approach

- Determine your preferred philosophy from among the strategies of power running, quick hitting, option attack, misdirection, or some combination.

- Select three to four running plays you feel match the talent ability of your team, and plan to learn them to perfection.

- Anticipate those critical situations in which your basic plays could become stopped by the defense and select two to three other plays you can fall back on. For Example, a reverse, counter, throwback, etc.

"Keep it Simple"

Offensive Formations and Strategies

Formation Selection Approach

- Select the formation which best fits your talent and play selection. For example, a power running game is better suited from a Power-I than a Pro Slot, because you need the backs in the blocking scheme.

- Take the core set of plays and execute them to perfection with repetition, repetition and more repetition, until footwork, timing, position, and hand-offs become second nature.

- If the play is successful, run it until the defense stops it.

- If the play is unsuccessful, don't abandon it until you have analyzed what adjustments can be made to make it successful.

- Add a second formation, if necessary, to run your special plays, or provide a different look to the defense, yet, keep your same blocking schemes.

- Include at least two simple pass plays in your scheme. Some of the simpler, yet effective ones are the sprint out, the slant-in to a split end or flanker, and a tight end dump off pass.

- Use a strong type formation to outnumber the defenders on one side of the center. For example, I-Formation with a tight wingback.

- A commonly used strategy combines the following plays:

  - Quick hit inside,   ~22 Blast, 31 Blast~
  - Power off tackle,   ~46 Dive~   ~44 Cutback~
  - Toss sweep,   ~37 Sweep, 38 option~
  - Misdirection, like the counter or cross buck, and   ~41 Counter~
  - ~PASS~ Quarterback keep.   ~PA PASS, The Fly~

  This combination allows you to attack any part of the field.

Learning The Hard Way: *"The Oversized Playbook"*

Stay with a **minimum** number of plays and drill them to perfection. Avoid continuously adding more and more plays. The more plays you introduce, the greater the learning curve becomes. I learned this lesson many years ago. I coached an extremely talented and undefeated team throughout the season. About mid-season, I began adding one to two plays per week, and the team kept learning and executing. By season's end, our playbook numbered fifteen to twenty different types of plays and four to five formations. I couldn't even remember them all! In the championship game, we had to struggle to beat a far less talented team, only because we had become too diversified. After the game, it

Learning The Hard Way: *"The Oversized Playbook," continued*

was obvious we had lost our effectiveness on the core plays by attempting so many additional ones. There's an old saying in football, "Go with what Brung You!" In other words, execute what you can do best and stick with it. I ditched the playbook and never made that mistake again!

Now that you have a grasp of how the offensive attack is organized, let's take a look at some of the many types of formations used in the game. Trust me, these illustrations just scratch the surface.

 ## The Single Wing

This was one of the original offensive formations utilized during the origins of the game. The alignment of the deepest to the shallowest back forms a line similar to a wing. The backs align to one side of the offense; thus, the name single wing. It often employed an unbalanced line as well, so in effect, you had the defense on that side of the ball totally outnumbered. The strategy was to deep snap the ball to the most talented back(s) who would follow lead blocking backs and/or pulling linemen into, or around the line of scrimmage. The downside is that the formation signals where the play is going. It can still be a useful formation if the defense is fixed or caught off guard. Again, the strategy is to outnumber the defenders at the point of attack. Don't laugh it off; I've sprinkled it in to my offenses repeatedly with great success. My only variation is to have the quarterback take the snap from underneath the center, rather than deep snap to a back, which is harder to do for the younger players. This type of running play is often referred to as "Power" football.

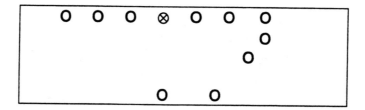

 ## The Double Wing

Today's double wing employs a running back at each wing with a quarterback underneath the center, and one deep running back, typically in the I-Formation behind the Quarterback. The formation provides a diverse range of points of attack. The strategy is to use a wing back in motion to decoy the defense, while using the other backs to run counters, traps and pass routes along with the tight ends. Key requirements are that the offensive lineman must have the skills to pull and trap, and all the players must remember a multitude of assignments. When executed properly, it can be one of the most difficult formations to defense.

Offensive Formations and Strategies

The Double Wing, *continued*

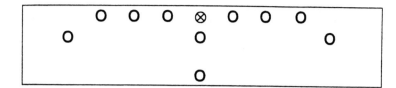

A Pro Set Wing

One set that illustrates the Pro Type formations is with a split end, a flanker on the opposite side, and two split running backs. Obviously, this enables the offense to spread the defense and threaten with both the pass and run. It requires a solid proficiency of line blocking, since at least two to three of your eleven players will consistently run pass routes, which may reduce your ability to stop aggressive defenses.

A Pro Set Double Slot

This formation employs four possibly five receivers, if you run a back out of the backfield into the flat, or underneath the linebacker coverage. Teams with a talented quarterback, speedy receivers and a super running back can afford to use this formation. This is obviously a pass oriented offense.

Split Backs Veer Formation

This formation is referred to as a belly series, which means the quarterback inserts the ball into a running backs belly, and either gives it or pulls it away if he sees the opportunity to run off tackle or around the end. The formation is a variation of the Triple Option Wishbone, with an additional threat of the pass play. This is accomplished by using one of the backs at the flanker, or slot position, who typically poses a pass threat to the secondary on the side of the play. The pass threat from the flanker, or slot, helps to slow the reaction of secondary defenders who must aid the defensive line to stop the quarterback who can handoff, run or pitch to a trailing back. This offense requires speed and flawless execution of techniques by the quarterback and running backs.

Offensive Formations and Strategies

- Formation

This may be the best offensive set to teach youth players, and ironically, it evolved from the Single Wing. As you can see from the backs alignment, you can attack the defense with straight ahead runs, often referred to as "Quicks," at any point along the defensive line of scrimmage. As you will see in the playbook, it also provides the opportunities to run counters, sweeps, and power runs with other backs as lead blockers. Finally, it's flexible enough to execute passing with one or two backs blocking and the other back joining the pass routes.

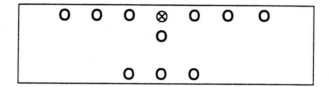

The I Formation

The I-Formation attempts to add more passing capability by using one of the backs as a flanker, and a split end on the opposite side. The alignment can spread the defense and increase the success of running, as well. The formation permits straight ahead "Quicks," with the fullback, or the tailback, counters with the tailback or flanker, and power running, with the fullback lead blocking for the tailback. Since two of the running backs are aligned directly behind the quarterback, it allows you to attack both sides of the line of scrimmage with equal quickness.

Summary

- Offensive formations and strategies can range from simple to extremely complex. Keep it simple in youth football, because the objective is learning.

- The overall strategy has to be matched to the level of the talent. Evaluate the ability of your team, then select a formation which compliments them.

- Consider alternatives to teaching methods, but don't lose sight of the fact there is a universal system of X's and O's used to teach the game at higher levels.

- Pick a strategy that is simple and stay with it.

- Communicate the strategy to the team and the parents.

- Don't panic about having to develop formations and plays; this manual has them for you.

Defensive Formations and Strategies

 Objectives

The objectives in this chapter are:

1. Understand basic defensive formations and common terminology

2. Review several fundamental youth defensive alignments

3. Tips on developing your individual defensive strategy

Like the offensive side of the game, there are many defenses, and each was created with a strategy in mind. As offenses evolved, defenses were created to stop them. Like the offense, youth defense should be kept as simple as possible. In the youth age groups, there is no need to make it more complicated than necessary, and I'm going to offer you a simplified approach.

Before selecting your defense, let's look at the basic position alignments and what they are intended to accomplish. Like the offense, defenses also have some common designations for alignment, which focus on:

1. The areas along the line of scrimmage called "gaps" or "holes"

2. Areas of the field beyond the line of scrimmage, called "zones," and

3. "Man-to-man" coverage for defending against a specific offensive player

 Defensive Formation Designations

The first set of designations applies to the defensive players opposite the offensive linemen on the line of scrimmage. Unlike the offensive rules, the defense can place as many players as desired on the line of scrimmage. However, the common approaches typically employ some combination of the following: a nose guard opposite the center, defensive guards in front of the offensive guards, defensive tackles in front of the tackles, and a defensive end in front of the offensive end. In other words, the defensive attempts to match player for player, for <u>most</u> of the offensive line positions. Defensive formations are typically labeled by a double number, or simply a name. For example: (a) "6-2" Indicates six defensive linemen, two linebackers, and the other three defenders are corners, and/or safeties, although not specified in the number; (b) "5-2" Indicates five defensive linemen, two linebackers, and two corner backs and two safeties; (c) "Seven Diamond" Indicates seven defensive linemen, one linebacker in the middle, who forms a diamond configuration with the two cornerbacks and the one safety.

Finally, defenses are often labeled as "Even" or "Odd," simply based on how many players are on the defensive line of scrimmage.

Defensive Formations and Strategies

 ## Position Alignments

Alpha characters, or **terms,** are typically used to designate where the defensive linemen should attack to counter the offensive block. *Older age groups, primarily high school and above, will utilize numbering and terms such as "Technique," which aligns the defender straight up on either shoulder, or in the gap of the offensive line. For Youth Football, stay with simple numbering and lettering. Technique is generally far too advanced for youth players.*

Defensive linemen are lined up in a down three or four point stance either directly over (*"Head Up/Nose to Nose"*), *nose* on one of the *shoulders*, or *nose* in the *gap,* depending on the defensive coaching philosophy. Let's look at the logic behind those alignments.

1. Nose-to-nose aids the defender to fight, or control, the blocker to either side. It also allows the defender to use more of the defensive techniques we discussed in Chapter 6, such as the forearm shiver.

2. Nose-in-the-gap allows the defender to get through the opening quickly and plug that area against the run. It also forces the blocker to move laterally to protect that gap, and it may not be the way he intended to block. On the other hand, it is easier for the offensive lineman to push the defender out of an area.

3. Nose-on-the-shoulder allows the defender to protect one side of the hole, while maintaining some ability to move back across the facemask of the blocker, to the other side, if necessary.

If players are instructed to attack the gaps, simple letter designations are commonly used as shown below:

DEFENSIVE DESIGNATION BY GAPS

End	C	B	A	A	B	C	End
↓	O↓	O↓	O↓	⊗↓	O↓	O↓	O↓
				①			
		②		③		④	

DEFENSIVE DESIGNATION OF "HEAD UP"

X	X	X		X	X	X
O	O	O	⊗	O	O	O
			①			
	②		③		④	

When you determine how many players will be along the line of scrimmage, you can designate some, or all, to attack, using the above lettering. Caution, although there are infinite combinations which can be changed every play, try to stay <u>consistent,</u> in order to facilitate learning and avoid confusion.

Position Alignments, *continued*

Linebackers are generally positioned about a yard behind the defensive linemen in an upright, or breakdown position. Together with the cornerbacks and safety, they form a secondary line of defense. They can be positioned anywhere along the defensive line of scrimmage, based on the responsibilities you assign them. If your opponent has a strong running game to the outside, you may wish to position them around the defensive tackle and end, so that they can pursue outside more quickly to aid in stopping the run. On the other hand, if your opponent has a balanced attack and runs inside as well, you may wish to line them up closer to the center, to allow them to cover laterally in both directions, as well as straight ahead. You can use the same designations as for the defensive linemen, in stopping the run. To defend against the pass, the terms "zone" and "man-to-man" are commonly used. The following diagram illustrates field zones both laterally and perpendicular to the line of scrimmage. Linebackers are generally responsible for defending these areas against the run and the pass.

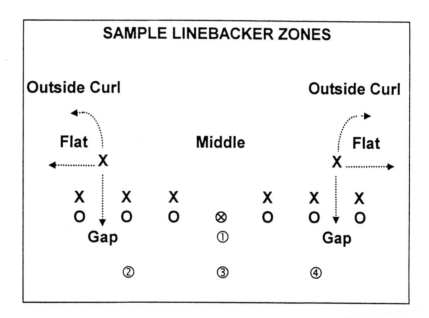

Defenses are designed to utilize the linebackers, cornerbacks, safeties, and often the defensive ends, to provide protection of zones from sideline to sideline, and all the way to the defender's goal line. Don't panic yet, this will all become clearer as you view some of the defenses illustrated in the following sections!

Basic Defensive Theory. Simply put, the key to any defensive formation is to align your players to protect the area of the field you believe the offense will attack. Obviously, offenses are going to use running backs to attack through holes or gaps created by the offensive lineman, run around the end, or advance the ball through the air with a forward pass. Therefore, defenses have evolved to deploy their eleven players in a formation which can stop attacks in these areas, as referenced earlier.

Position Alignments, *continued*

Defenses may have an advantage in that the rules of the game don't require a certain number of players in any one area. For example, if you face a team which cannot execute the forward pass, theoretically you could align all eleven defenders on, or up to, the line of scrimmage, and outnumber the offense considerably.

However, experience proves that most teams need some level of secondary protection to stop the back who gets through, or around the line of scrimmage, and also be able to defend an opponent who can successfully execute the forward pass. **Fortunately for the youth coach, there are some basic, commonly used formations which are effective and simple to teach.**

Common Defensive Formations. A quick word about defensive formations. Different formations are used to stop certain types of offensive attacks, as previously mentioned. If you've got the experience and expertise, there are many formations from which to choose. However, for youth football, I recommend using simple **rules of thumb**.

Rule # 1   Utilize a defense that "mirrors" the offensive formation. In other words, if the offensive backfield is evenly distributed, such as the Straight-T, or Wishbone, align your defense to provide the same balance of player distribution, so that you have an equal number of players to attack each area of the field, inside and out, and not be disadvantaged by more offensive players.

Rule #2   If the offensive formation is strong to one side with a flanker/wingback or additional slot backs and wide receivers, adjust your balance to the same side by using one of the safeties, often referred to as strong safety. This provides a way to counter the additional offensive players on a particular side of the offensive formation. Let's look at some common defensive alignments:

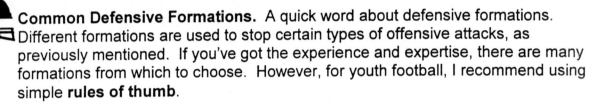

6-2 "TIGHT"
Good balance against outside and inside running!

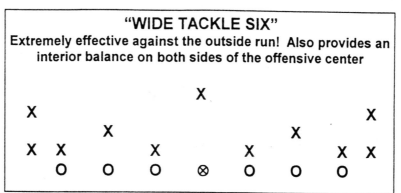

"WIDE TACKLE SIX"
Extremely effective against the outside run! Also provides an interior balance on both sides of the offensive center

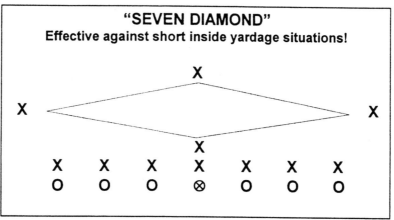

"SEVEN DIAMOND"
Effective against short inside yardage situations!

5-2 "OKLAHOMA"
Excellent overall balance against running and passing!

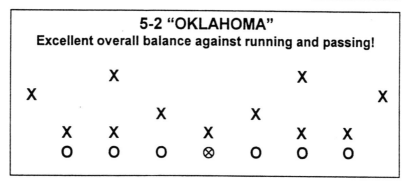

5-2 "OKLAHOMA" VS. "POWER I"
Notice the "Strong Safety ⊙ " positioned to equal the balance to that side

X - Free Safety

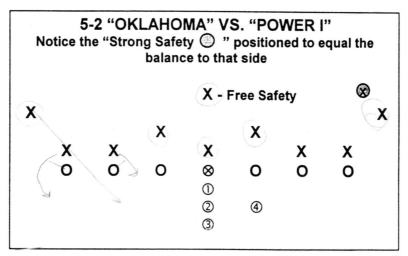

Defensive Formations and Strategies

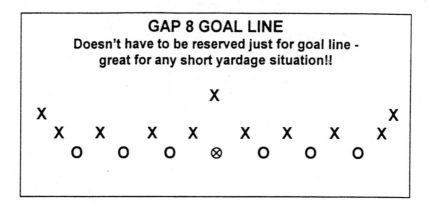

GAP 8 GOAL LINE
Doesn't have to be reserved just for goal line -
great for any short yardage situation!!

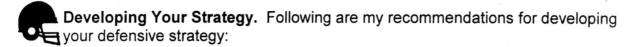

 Developing Your Strategy. Following are my recommendations for developing your defensive strategy:

- First, check your league rules to determine what flexibility you have. Some organizations require strict rules on what type of alignment is permitted. This is done as a way to facilitate learning through simplicity, and ensuring that teams are not significantly disadvantaged in their ability to compete. This is a philosophy I really support.

- Select a defensive formation with at least six players on the line of scrimmage. Two very effective formations are the 6-2 "Tight" and the "Wide Tackle Six." Both formations utilize a single defensive safety. Your number one priority in <u>most</u> youth leagues is to stop the run. However, in those rare situations when your opponent is a strong passing team, you will, of course, have to adjust. In that situation, I recommend using the 5-2 "Oklahoma," which utilizes two safeties.

- Select the top five most talented players for key positions. The criteria should be:

  a) **knowledge** of the game   c) **desire/aggressiveness**
  b) **tackling** ability   d) **quickness**

- Position <u>two</u> at the defensive ends. Position <u>one</u> at linebacker, and <u>one</u> at cornerback, both on the strong side of the offensive attack. Position <u>one</u> player at an inside guard. What you have just done is to form a solid perimeter which defends both the outside, and inside run.

- Select a solid performer to be positioned at safety. Break the paradigm that your fastest back has to play that position. If your team has to depend on that position to make the plays, you've got some serious defensive problems up front!

Defensive Formations and Strategies

☞ Decide how you want your guards and tackles to attack, either the gap, control, or a combination. If you want to use a combination of "Control" and "Gap" as discussed in Chapter 5, I recommend tackles head up, and the guard attacking the "A Gap." The linebacker protects the "B Gap." Periodically switch their assignments to head up, or the opposite gap.

☞ Use "Stunts" <u>occasionally</u> and keep them simple. Too many and too complicated will confuse your players, and result in big gains for the offense.

☞ Finally, I recommend using the "Box" defense for ages seven to ten. The concept here is to rush your defensive ends into the backfield, equal to the deepest offensive back, and force the outside sweep, counters, and traps back towards the interior line of scrimmage, where there are more defensive players to make the tackle. The "Box" defense is Illustrated below:

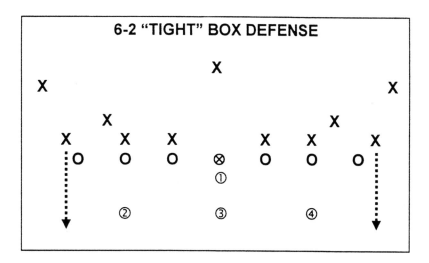

Obviously, the theory is to limit the lateral movement of the running backs. This requires that the defensive end's number one priority is to turn the running back inside. <u>However</u>, older players are likely to be taught a different approach, once reaching junior or high school levels. At that level, they may be required to move laterally toward the sidelines to turn the running back inside. This technique is required because of the higher level requirements for the corners and safeties in pass defense coverage. At that level of play, the defensive end begins to learn to play more like an outside linebacker, than the typical youth defensive end. Therefore, for your older players, I recommend you at least acquaint them with the difference in techniques.

Defensive Formations and Strategies

Summary

- In teaching defense, use simple terminology to describe your formations and areas of defensive responsibility: "6-2" alignment, "Gap A", "B" or "C", zones and man-to-man, for pass protection.

- If you know what type of offensive formation you will be defending, consider using a defensive formation that mirrors the offense relative to balance across the field.

- As a rule, use at least six players on the defensive line of scrimmage, and focus on stopping the run.

- Be conservative in the use of stunts, and the frequency with which you change gap, or head up responsibilities.

- Spend time ensuring your players understand the terminology, and their key responsibilities play after play.

- Don't be afraid to switch to a more aggressive defense, such as the "Seven Diamond" or "Gap 8." Just make sure you have practiced it sufficiently beforehand.

- Finally, keep those running backs from getting outside. The "Box" approach is an excellent philosophy to use.

There's not a season goes by without many coaches being quoted: "Defenses Win The Big Games!" You need to be the judge of that saying.

Practice Plans

 ## Practice Sessions

This chapter provides a sample, or go-by, for organizing your practice sessions, tips on certain areas of focus, and illustrated stretching techniques to begin the team warm-ups. The first week of suggested activities is provided to develop a foundation for the many weeks to come. The suggested time per activity will obviously have to be adjusted to fit your individual situation.

During that first week it is absolutely critical to set the expectations for the players' participation, behavior, team rules, etc. Second, motivate them into looking forward to the season. Third, establish an adequate orientation to the offensive fundamentals, and last, begin evaluating how you will utilize the talent on the team. Before the first practice session begins, you should have a plan for how the first few weeks of the season should progress. Don't make the mistake of going day-by-day, or week-by-week! Have a plan; it doesn't materialize the way you expected, you can always adjust.

Following are some tips on how to plan the season's progress.

- Review Chapter 1 and develop your weekly plans, in accordance with the F.A.S.T. model.

- Scout your opponents, and dedicate practice time to executing specific strategies.

- Continuously evaluate your players and your offensive and defensive strategies. While it's not desirable to make mid-season changes, it may be necessary if you matched the wrong player to the wrong position, and a player develops later in the season. Relative to your strategy, changing mid-season could cause more harm than good, but it is always worth considering if you are not having success.

- Practice injury management with prevention, identification and appropriate treatment. Use preventive techniques, such as well designed warm-up and cool-down periods. Ensure your coaches are teaching safety first in all their techniques, and monitoring such throughout practices. Treat every injury seriously. Some injuries can be self-managed through Rest, Ice, Compression and Elevation (R.I.C.E.), while others should be treated by a qualified medical professional. Review the safety tips from the American Red Cross!

- Design your practices so that position skills continue to advance week-by-week. Don't forget to establish early season individual goals for each player's skill development.

- Finally, plan your practice sessions in advance, do them as you planned, and measure the results.

Drills which apply to specific activities will be noted with a ◯ *and drill number.*

"Planning and Organizing Are Keys To Teaching"

Practice Plans

Practice Sessions, *continued*

Day 1 - Objectives: Assumes Separate Parent Meeting

1. Getting to know each other, orientation to season objectives, rules, etc.	4. Begin evaluating speed and agility for determining best suited position(s)
2. Begin light conditioning	5. Begin teaching, ensuring players understand the fundamentals of the game
3. Begin learning offensive techniques of stances	6. Have fun!

Always include sufficient water breaks!

TIME	ACTIVITIES	COACH'S NOTES
15	Introductions and agreement on **"Ground Rules"** and the basics of the F.A.S.T. model, see Chapter 1	
5	Overview of Week 1, and what players can expect to do and learn	
15	Equipment check and other administrative details, as required by the league	
20	Warm-ups: short lap at half speed to loosen the muscles, jogging in place; jumping jacks; stretches; pushups	
10	Motion Drills ⑨	
15	Run zig-zags through cones with a football; ⑫ run toss-sweeps from the I back position	
30	Stances; explain the purpose of angles and thrust ①	

"Planning and Organizing Are Keys To Teaching"

Practice Plans

Practice Sessions, *continued*

Day 1 - Objectives, Assumes Separate Parent Meeting, *continued*

TIME	ACTIVITIES	COACH'S NOTES
30	Begin instruction on fundamentals of the game. Review the objectives, the Offense vs. the Defense, use the illustrations in the Playbook. Sprints Cool Downs 5 - 30 yard 3 - 20 yard 3 - 20 yard 2 - 10 yard 2 - 20 yard	
10	De-brief Did everyone have fun? Plans for Day 2 Any bumps, bruises, blisters, etc.? Team yell and dismiss Recap the practice learnings	

NOTES

Practice Plans

Practice Sessions, *continued*

Day 2 - Objectives:

1. Continue light conditioning	4. **Begin teaching the fundamentals of the planned offensive formation**
2. Continue learning 3 and 4 point stances	5. **Have fun!**
3. Continue evaluating speed and agility for determining best suited position(s). Identify and begin work with potential quarterbacks and centers	

Always include sufficient water breaks!

TIME	ACTIVITIES	COACH'S NOTES
15	Warm-ups: short lap, stretches; jogging in place; jumping jacks; pushups; other.	
10	Motion drills ⑨	
10	Run zig-zags through cones, with a football; run toss sweeps from the I back position ⑫	
15	Stances ①	
40	Break into three instruction groups: 1. QB's - center snap, cadence, footwork and ball handling ② 2. Center's ② 3. Linemen fundamentals - Blocking Dummy ③	

"Planning and Organizing Are Keys To Teaching"

Practice Plans

Practice Sessions, *continued*

Day 2 - Objectives:

TIME	ACTIVITIES	COACH'S NOTES
30	Continue instruction on fundamentals of the game: Review the objectives for the offense, using illustrations of the team's planned offensive formation and 1-2 plays. Line the team up in the offensive formation; teach the positions, hole numbers, and assignments.	
20	Sprints 5 - 30 yard 3 - 20 yard 2 - 20 yard Cool Downs 3 - 20 yard 2 - 10 yard	
10	De-brief Did everyone have fun? Any bumps, bruises, blisters, etc.? Recap the practice learnings Plans for Day 3 Team yell and dismiss	

NOTES

Practice Plans

Practice Sessions: - *Continued*

Day 3 - Objectives:

1. Continue light conditioning	4. **Select the "first pass" of potential running backs and linemen**
2. **Continue learning 3 and 4 point stances and drive blocking against blocking dummies**	5. **Continue the fundamentals of the planned offensive formation. Introduce the planned primary defensive alignment**
3. Begin learning proper tackling techniques	6. Have fun!

Always include sufficient water breaks!

TIME	ACTIVITIES
15	Warm-ups: short lap, stretches; jogging in place; jumping jacks; pushups; other.
10	Motion drills ⑨
10	Stances ①
40	Break into two instruction groups: 1. Running Backs ⑪ ⑫ ⑬ 2. Linemen fundamentals - 3 Step Approach To Blocking ③ ④ ⑤
20	Tackling Techniques ⑰ ⑱
20	Line the team up in the offensive and defensive formations, and repeat the learning from Day 2 for 1-3 plays.

"Planning and Organizing Are Keys To Teaching"

Practice Plans

Practice Sessions, *continued*

Day 3 - Objectives, *continued*

TIME	ACTIVITIES	COACH'S NOTES
15	TAG Sprints: see Chapter 1 Cool Downs 3 - 20 yard 2 - 10 yard	
10	De-brief Did everyone have fun? Any bumps, bruises, blisters, etc.? Re-cap the practice learnings	Plans for Day 4 Team yell and dismiss

NOTES

Practice Plans

"Planning and Organizing Are Keys To Teaching"

Practice Plans

Practice Sessions, *continued*

Day 4 - Objectives:

1. Live contact in blocking and tackling	4. Introduce basic rules of the game
2. Continued learning of skill positions for running backs and linemen	5. Have fun!
3. Execute 2 - 4 offensive plays against a live defensive alignment	

Always include sufficient water breaks!

TIME	ACTIVITIES	COACH'S NOTES
15	Warm-ups: short lap, stretches; jogging in place; jumping jacks; pushups; other.	
10	Motion drills - fumble recoveries - using "Fetus" technique ⑨	
40	Break into two instruction groups: 1. Running backs ⑪ ⑬ ⑭ 2. QB and center exchange ② 3. Linemen fundamentals ③ ⑥	
30	Tackling techniques ⑰ ⑱	
30	Line the team up in the offensive and defensive formations, and repeat the learning from Day 3 for 2 - 4 plays. Walk through the assignments and run a <u>few</u> of the plays live against the defense.	

"Planning and Organizing Are Keys To Teaching"

Practice Plans

Practice Sessions, *continued*

Day 4 - Objectives, *continued*

TIME	ACTIVITIES	COACH'S NOTES
20	Tag Sprints Run a lap 3 - 20 yard Cool Downs 2 - 10 yard 5 - 30 yard <u>Stretches!</u>	
10	De-brief Did everyone have fun? Plans for Day 5 Any bumps, bruises, blisters, etc.? Team yell and dismiss Re-cap the practice learnings	

NOTES

Practice Plans

Practice Sessions, *continued*

Day 5 - Objectives:

1. Live contact in blocking and tackling	4. Introduce basic rules of the game
2. Continued learning of skill positions for running backs and linemen	5. Have fun!
3. Execute 2 - 4 offensive plays against a live defensive alignment	

Always include sufficient water breaks!

TIME	ACTIVITIES	COACH'S NOTES
15	Warm-ups: short lap, stretches; jogging in place; jumping jacks; pushups; other.	
30	Break into two instruction groups: 1. Running backs ⑪ ⑬ ⑭ ⑮ 2. QB and center exchange ② 3. Linemen fundamentals ③ ⑤ ⑥ ⑧	
20	Tackling techniques ⑰ ⑱	
30	Line the team up in the offensive formation and repeat the learning from Day 4 for 2 - 4 plays. Run the basic plays without a defense. Focus on the huddle, proper alignment of the offensive line, and the neutral zone, and the cadence.	
30	Line the team up in the primary defensive formation, and walk through the position assignments. Utilize visual aids to demonstrate the objectives. Emphasize the **Three Step Approach To Defensive Play (SSS)** Chapter 5.	

"Planning and Organizing Are Keys To Teaching"

Practice Plans

Practice Sessions, *continued*

Day 5 - Objectives, *continued*

TIME	ACTIVITIES	COACH'S NOTES
15	Run light lap Walk a lap Stretch Review rules, infractions	
10	De-brief Did everyone have fun? Any bumps, bruises, blisters, etc.? Re-cap the practice learnings	Plans for Day 6 (Live Scrimmage!) Team yell and dismiss

NOTES

Practice Plans

"Planning and Organizing Are Keys To Teaching"

Practice Plans

Practice Sessions, *continued*

Day 6 - Objectives:

1. **Becoming a team, "road to the season"**	4. **Recap of week 1**
2. **Fun drills**	5. **Have fun!**
3. **Offensive plays against a live defensive alignment**	

Always include sufficient water breaks!

TIME	ACTIVITIES	COACH'S NOTES
15	Warm-ups: light lap, stretches	
15	Hand-off relay races, fumble relay race	
15	Reviewing offensive and defensive formations and objectives, using visual aids, alignments and walk throughs	
60	Scrimmage: run the primary offense vs the primary defense. Rotate players so that everyone gets offense and defense participation	
15	Team run - see Chapter 1 Cool Downs 3 - 20 yard <u>Stretches!</u> 5 - 30 yard	
15	De-brief - F.A.S.T. emphasis on becoming a team • Recognition on good first week effort • Begin discussing requirements each player must develop; personal goals for the season; report out at the conclusion of Week #2 • Plans for Week 2 • Team yell and dismiss	

Stretches

Hip Flexor. Turn the body 90 degrees to right or left, and point both feet in the same direction. Step forward with the lead foot, bending the lead knee to 90 degrees to the ground, and the back leg/knee in a straightened position. Keep the upper torso erect as you stretch the rear hip. Reverse direction and stretch the other hip.

Calf. Lean against a partner, with the feet shoulder width apart and pointed slightly inward. Keep the feet flat on the ground, and move the hips inward toward the partner, stretching the calf muscles.

Quadriceps. Grasp the shoulder of a partner for balance. Grasp the ankle with the same side hand, and slowly stretch the foot toward the buttocks. Repeat with the opposite foot.

Stretches - *Continued*

Posterior Cuff. While standing upright, slowly stretch one arm across the upper torso to loosen the posterior area of the shoulder.

Shoulder and Chest. Place the arms behind the back, grabbing one wrist with the other hand. Raise the arms up slowly, while keeping the upper torso erect.

Trunk and Hip Rotation. In a seated position, with the upper torso erect, keep one leg outstretched and straight on the ground. Cross the other leg over the outstretched knee, and place the foot flat on the ground. Place the elbow opposite the raised knee against the outside of the raised knee. Use the other arm back, with the hand on the ground. Slowly rotate the trunk. Repeat to the opposite side.

Stretches - *Continued*

Hamstring/Spread Eagle. In a sitting position, with legs spread apart, reach both arms toward the toes of either leg. Grab the toes and pull back slowly. Be sure to keep the knees slightly bent to avoid hyperextension of the knee.

Groin Adductors. While seated, keep the back straight, bend the knees out, and put the bottom of the feet against each other. Put the elbows on top of the knees and gently pull the feet toward the groin. Keep pressure on the knees, pushing them toward the ground.

Lower Back. Lie flat on the back with both legs outstretched, and on the ground. Pull one leg up to the chest, while keeping the other leg flat on the ground and straight. Repeat with the opposite leg.

Lower Back. Lie on the back with the knees bent to a 45 degree angle, and the feet flat on the ground. Wrap both hands around the knees, and slowly pull the knees up to the chest area, while keeping the head and back flat against the ground.

Drill Objectives

This chapter focuses on three primary objectives:

"Try to keep them moving and participating as much as possible!"

---

1. Any drill should have an objective which supports the development of a required skill, or one of the other three elements, Fun, Attitude or Teamwork.

2. Some drills should be practiced throughout the season, while others may only be needed at a certain stage of the team's development.

3. Organize drills in a manner which includes repetition, individual evaluation and continuous participation. Station drills are some of the more traditional and effective methods. Establish two to three stations where a drill is taught to develop different techniques. After 10 to 15 minutes, rotate the players to the next station. Another effective method is to teach the same drill, but divide the players up into two to three groups, so each player can receive more repetitions. Whenever possible, avoid having players standing around, waiting for their turn.

4. Learning a skill can be significantly improved using two techniques:

    A. Use the "Fit" position, which is the name of a commonly used technique in football. It means to physically place the player into the final position, or technique being taught. For example, to teach the shoulder block, begin by placing the blocker against the defender in the proper position, so they understand the fundamentals required. Continue by separating the players, and increasing the distance between them, until the drill is executed from the proper stance, or alignment. Many refer to this as teaching the skill in the reverse order.

    B. Use half speed or limited resistance, as often as possible. Repetition is the key to learning. If both opponents are going at it full speed, it's difficult to execute properly with each repetition. Half speed also reduces the risk of injury during practices.

Drills

How To Use This Section

🐦 Remember each drill is numbered to cross reference it to a preceding chapter. The Whistle icons are numbered to reference an ascending order from Chapter 3 forward.

🐦 Recognize what each symbol represents.

🐦 Focus on the desired development of each drill, and follow the numbered steps.

🐦 Don't hesitate to vary these drills. If you have a better method, just be sure your desired outcome is intended to develop, and improve the player's ability.

Symbols

Δ	= Cone	©	= Offensive Center
O	= Offensive Blocker	●	= Football
■	= Blocking Dummy	C	= Coach
X	= Defensive Player	●	= Ball Carrier

Drills

 ## 1 3 and 4 Point Stances

Desired Development: balance, weight distribution, coil-like striking ability, head and eyes up .

Steps:

1. Line groups of 4-5 side-by-side.
2. Work them individually to develop the technique.
3. Have them fire out over, and to both sides of the cone.
4. Teach stepping and bringing the body forward, with the arms coming up to form the shoulder block technique, one continuous motion.

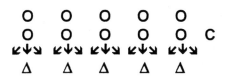

"Elbows Out/Palms Down"
Sprint Five Yards & Return to back of line

 ## 2 Center Snap

Desired Development: good stance, head and eyes up, one or two handed snap, quick movement w/snap of the ball.

Steps:

1. Work the stance over the ball.
2. Work the hand snap w/out the ball. Center's hand comes up to slap against QB's upper hand.
3. Work the snap with the ball.
4. Work snap and movement simultaneously with upright blocking dummy. Get a rhythm established!

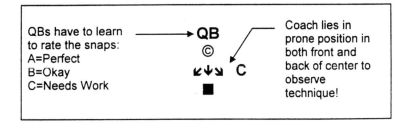

Drills

 ### 3 Drive Block

Desired Development: good stance, fire forward, hard thrust in both the upper sternum and the belt buckle approach, role those hips and upright the defender, head up and eyes up, feet wide and drive w/quick choppy steps.

Steps:

1. Teach the three step approach.
2. Begin with blocking dummy.
3. Live one-on-one with players in "fit" approach, physically against each other, using limited resistance to begin.
4. Progress to half-speed, then full-speed.
5. Emphasize stepping with rear foot when defender is over, and near foot when defender is to side, or gap.
6. *Repeat the drill using the hand techniques; hands to sternum, arms inside the frame of the body.*

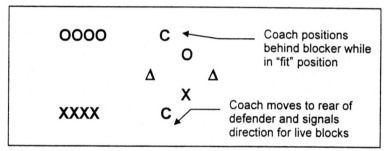

 ### 4 Double Team Block

Desired Development: understanding post and pivot responsibilities, hips together, for "wedge," elbows out/palms down, head and eyes up, feet wide, driving out of the hole, and down the line of scrimmage.

Steps:

1. Review the responsibilities.
2. Begin the players in the "fit" position.
3. Execute live at half speed, then full speed.
4. Rotate the players, so that each learns the post and the pivot.

"Success is driving the defender outside of the cones"

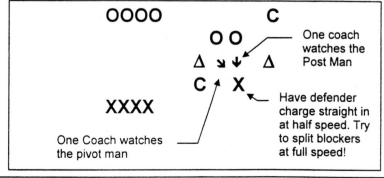

Pull and Trap Block

Desired Development: good stance without pointing, back and lateral step w/direction foot, use of the elbow to pull body around and into direction, contact with the backside shoulder to kick defender out.

Steps:

1. Ensure proper stance.
2. Execute to outside.
3. Make contact against upright dummy.
4. Work live against defender with a hand held dummy.
5. Work live against defender without a blocking dummy.
6. Work to the opposite side, and against interior defensive linemen.
7. *Remember the rules for blocking below the waist!*

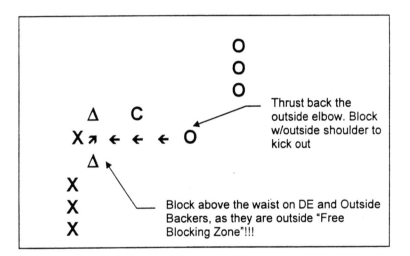

 ## "Blocking On The BoardWalk"

Desired Development: keeping feet shoulder-width apart while blocking; maintaining body contact; driving the opponent off the line of scrimmage.

Steps:

1. Use a hardwood plank/board 2"x 6" in width, and 10'-15' in length.
2. Mark the board in yard increments.
3. Align a blocker vs. a defender, head up.
4. On the snap count, the blocker must drive the defender down the board, without touching the board with his feet.
5. Begin half speed in the "fit" position, in which the defender allows blocker to execute the technique.
6. Run the drill live, with the objective of the blocker driving the defender at least three to five yards down the board.

"Blocking On The BoardWalk," *continued*

7. Any player who touches the board with his feet is penalized two yards, and the drill must be re-started.
8. Rules: straight-up blocking, with no side-steps, spins, or other evasive defensive techniques.

**Great challenge course!
Use the opportunity for recognition and awards!**

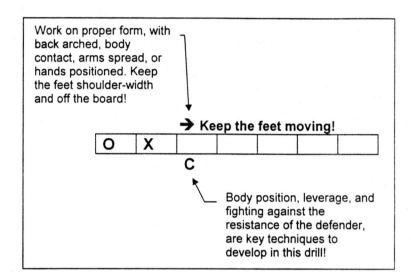

Work on proper form, with back arched, body contact, arms spread, or hands positioned. Keep the feet shoulder-width and off the board!

➔ **Keep the feet moving!**

Body position, leverage, and fighting against the resistance of the defender, are key techniques to develop in this drill!

 **7 The L.S.U. "V"**

Desired Development: downfield blocking by the offensive lineman, and techniques by the running back.

Steps:

1. Place two defenders at five yard intervals; they must attempt to tackle the running back <u>ABOVE</u> the waist.
2. Blocking lineman leads the play, and uses downfield technique on first defender.
3. Running back uses evasive techniques against both defenders.
4. Expand the drill with an additional blocker, and a defender, as desired, but only at wider area of the "V."

(Provided by Coach Tommy Fairburn, former LSU defensive back)

The L.S.U. "V," *continued*

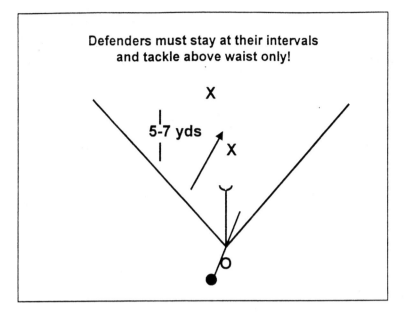

 "Oklahoma"

Desired Development: proper stance, sound blocking techniques, running back cuts to the open hole, sound defensive techniques.

Steps:
1. Align a blocker and a defender between two cones, with a running back at the normal backfield depth.
2. If practical, use a QB and center outside the cones, to hand-off to the running back.
3. Coach positions behind the defender and points to the gap, for the running back to attack and the snap count.
4. On the snap count, the blocker attempts to open the hole for the runner.
5. The defender plays straight up and learns to spot the runner, and slide into the hole, making the tackle.
6. Variations of the drill include adding a linebacker and/or other blockers and defensive linemen.

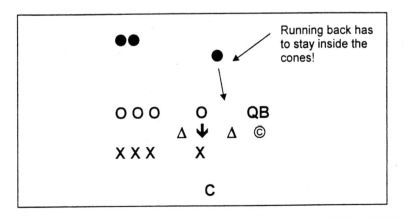

"Oklahoma," *continued*

- One of the best all around team drills ever developed! Practice it regularly!

- Vary the number of players and alignment.

- Try to utilize a coach per position if practical.

- Use this to work on defensive line techniques as well - Three Step Approach (Stop/Spot/Shed).

- Forearm block and hand shiver.

- Same opportunity applies for developing the linebacker techniques.

9 Motion Drill

Desired Development: proper breakdown stance, improved agility, footwork and directional movement, shoulders square to the line of scrimmage.

Steps:

1. Position one or more players side-by-side, facing the coach.
2. Coach holds a football and points it from side to side, straight forward, over his shoulder, varying the movement approximately every three to four seconds.
3. Players maintain breakdown stance, while moving the feet and pursuing in the direction of the ball, keeping the shoulders parallel to the coach, and line of scrimmage.
4. Keep the eyes on the ball at all times.
5. When finished, sprint to the back of the line.

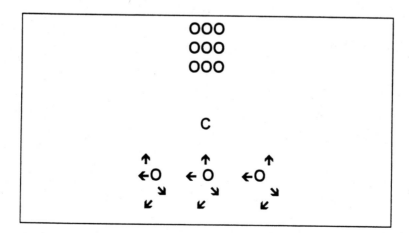

"Every Drill Should Produce A Desired Outcome!"

Drills

 Pass Blocking

Desired Development: execution of the both the "Play-Action" and the "Drop-Back" techniques; good initial contact and locking onto defender, assuming a proper set position, use of the hand shiver, locking onto the defender, and blocking out.

Steps:

1. Begin initial drill with players in set position - defender places hands on shoulder pads to push backward - blocker assumes good set position, with feet shoulder width, hands on defenders sternum pads, knees bent w/buttocks down, and back arched.
2. Have the players put resistance on each other and move laterally, shuffling their feet, with blocker staying in front of, and locked onto defender. Work backward, as well.
3. Work play-action first, with forward thrust and locking onto defender, as defender attempts to break into backfield, and reach the coach.
4. Make initial contact to upright the defender; then come up with the hands into the bottom of the chest protectors, with elbows inside frame of the body, and at 45 degree angle.
5. Have the defender attack straight through first, then to each side. Then have defender attempt to spin away from blocker to both sides. Blocker must lock onto/maintain contact with the defender, always fighting against the force of resistance.
6. Execute the drop-back protection.
7. Blocker drops inside, foot back, followed by other foot with toes even, buttocks dropped, back arched and hands in the ready position, to thrust into the defender.
8. Use the same defensive attack sequence, ending with the defender attempting to spin off, and the blocker maintaining position.
9. Finally, line up the entire offensive unit and work coverage at each position. Give the unit a goal, such as protection, for at least 4 seconds.

KEYS
- **Feet Shoulder Width**
- **Tail Down**
- **Back Arched**
- **Palms Up and Into Sternum**
- **Elbows 45 Degrees Below Shoulder/Inside Frame**
- **Stay Locked onto Defender**

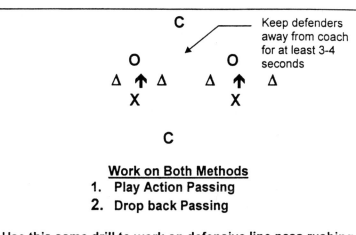

11 The Handoff

Desired Development: QB two hand technique, proper arm positioning for receiving handoff, protection of the ball when crossing line of scrimmage, protection of ball in open field running.

Steps:

1. Review two and three point stances for the running backs.
2. Review QB technique for holding the ball in his mid-section until time to reach the mid-section of running back.
3. Teach runner's arm positions for forming the "basket."
4. Coach hands off to each player, as they run a straight sprint to the line of scrimmage.
5. Repeat until techniques are acceptable; then have each player do the same with their eyes closed.
6. Have the QB execute the same steps including the fake and "Rock the Baby."
7. Finally, use relays to practice exchanges.

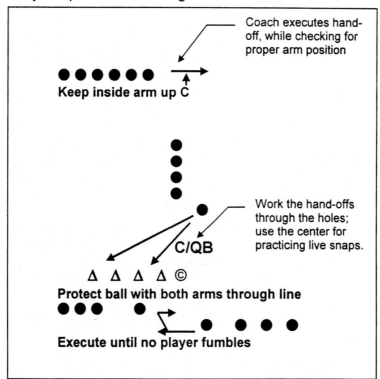

Hammer, Recover Drills and Tosses

Desired Development: maximum speed in open field running, maintaining balance and the "extra yard," watching the toss/pitch into the hands and tucking the ball.

Steps:

1. Align runners, side-by-side, and demonstrate using both hands to assimilate the hammer technique.
2. Runners perform half-speed sprint over 20-25 yds. On the whistle, fall forward, putting free hand on ground and pushing up to regain balance, without stumbling to ground.
3. QB pitches right and left to backs, who focus on fingers to sky, thumbs in, and eyes watching ball into grip, before tucking and running.

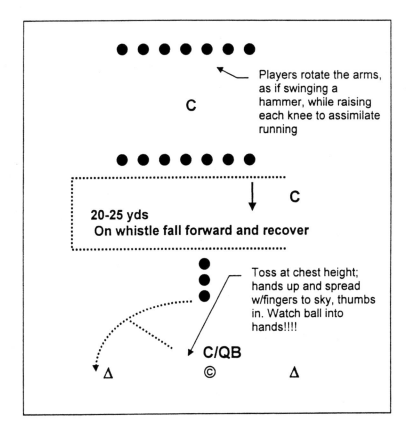

Drills

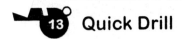

13 Quick Drill

Desired Development: proper running-back stance, hand-off execution, protecting the ball through the line of scrimmage, proper body position and running skills, upon contact at the line of scrimmage.

Steps:

1. Two defenders with hand held dummies, stand side by side on either side of the line of scrimmage hole, i.e. 2 hole.
2. Running-back takes the hand-off, and fires in between the defenders, against half to three quarter resistance.
3. Running-back maintains balance, shoulders to the line of scrimmage and a forward lean using his shoulders against the dummies assimilating running through a defender(s).
4. Running back must keep both hands/arms around the ball until past the defenders.
5. Once through the defenders, ball is placed against the rib cage in one arm and open field running begins for 5-10 yards.

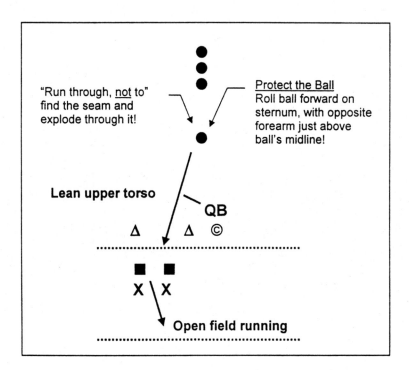

Drills

 14 Sideline Punch

Desired Development: learning the "punch" technique when pinned against the sideline, upward hook-like swing with inside arm into defenders sternum, along with thrust of shoulders, legs bent and hips used to move through the defender.

Steps:

1. Align 2-3 defenders with hand held dummies, beginning at a position outside the corner back, and near the sideline.
2. Running back takes the pitch and runs a sweep outside the defenders, and down the sideline.
3. Defenders attempt to push runner out of bounds, while runner uses "punch" technique to run through, and stay in bounds.

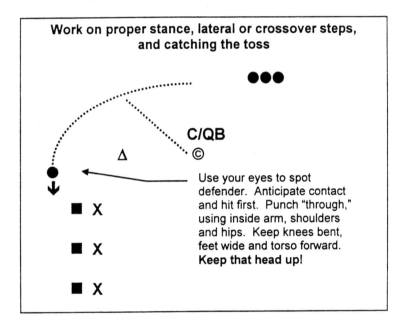

 15 Evasive Shuttle

Desired Development: open field running techniques of fake, crossover, and stiff arm.

Steps:

1. Set up three stations with upright blocking dummies, or live defenders.
2. Running backs move through each station, beginning at 3/4 speed, progressing to full speed after perfecting the technique.
3. Emphasize running with the eyes, keeping torso forward, using the plant/pivot foot, and locking the elbow during the stiff-arm.
4. Repeat the drill to the opposite side.

Evasive Shuttle, *continued*

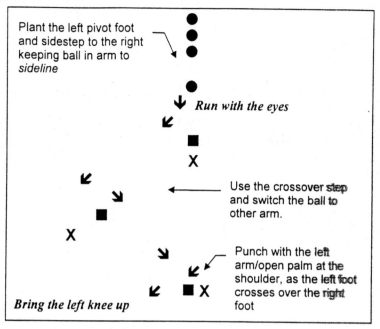

Plant the left pivot foot
and sidestep to the right
keeping ball in arm to
sideline

Run with the eyes

Use the crossover step
and switch the ball to
other arm.

Punch with the left
arm/open palm at the
shoulder, as the left foot
crosses over the right
foot

Bring the left knee up

 **16 Gauntlet**

Desired Development: power running through line of scrimmage by maintaining
balance, forward torso, widened legs, shoulders square, and ball protected.

Steps:

1. Place even number of defenders (8 or 10 preferred) on their knees facing each
   other approximately 1 and 1/2 yards apart side by side to the next defender.
2. Hand off to the Running back and require him to run through the gauntlet.
3. As he runs through, the kneeling players reach at his thighs, arms, hands, to
   throw him off balance and cause him to drop the ball.

**THE DEFENDERS ARE NOT PERMITTED TO GRAB AND HANG ON, MERELY
TO SWIPE AT RUNNER. SAFETY FIRST ABOVE ALL ELSE!!**

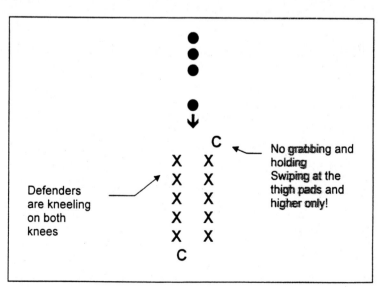

*Safety First - Don't get
runners hurt!*

No grabbing and
holding
Swiping at the
thigh pads and
higher only!

Defenders
are kneeling
on both
knees

Drills

 **Head On Tackle**

Desired Development: eyes on the mid-section, dropping the shoulders just prior to contact, facemask to the outside and into the ball, head up and back, arms wrapped around defender and into lower back, use of the legs to drive the defender up and to the ground.

Steps:

1. Align runners and tacklers opposite each other, and side by side, approximately two to three yards apart.
2. Assume the breakdown position, and on snap count, runner moves straight forward and tackler executes proper form.
3. Drill is always performed at 1/2 to 3/4 speed, to teach technique and avoid injury.
4. Coach critiques each tackler religiously, until technique is perfected.

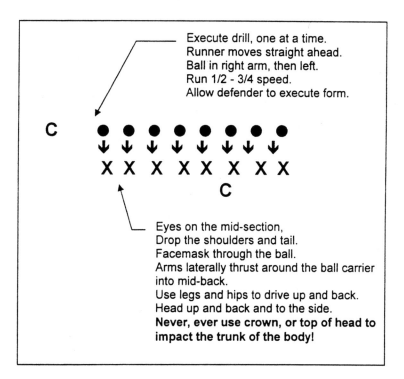

Drills

 **18** **Angle Tackle**

Desired Development: pursuit angles to intercept open field runners, targeting the point of contact, proper head placement, and fundamental tackling techniques.

Steps:

1. Align a runner and tackler across the line of scrimmage from each other.
2. Set up two cones approximately three to five yards down the line of scrimmage.
3. Assume the "breakdown" position; on the snap count, both players race for the cones.
4. As the back turns up through the cones, the defender makes the tackle.
5. Repeat the drill in both directions.

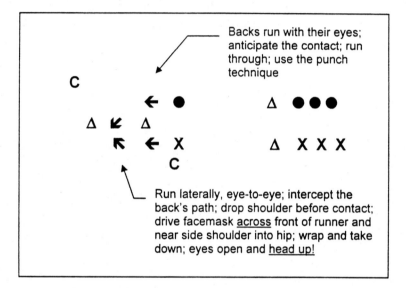

Drills

 **Box In Defense**

Desired Development: pursuit by the defensive end, corner back and linebacker, to force the outside sweep into the "box," defending against the reverse.

Steps:

1. Set up two cones, representing the offensive tight ends.
2. Align the offense with a center, quarterback, single I back, and the two offensive guards.
3. Align the defense with two defensive ends, two corners and two inside linebackers.
4. On the snap count, toss sweep to either side. Backside end, corner and linebacker should pursue, but are not allowed to help with the tackle. **This would obviously outnumber the runner and risk injury!**
5. Play side guard pulls and leads for the running back.
6. Defenders pursue to the appropriate position to force/make the play.
7. Backside defensive end **ensures no reverse before pursuing.**

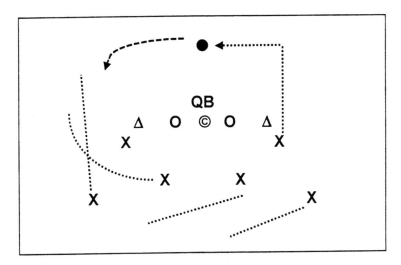

Stop Sweep Rules

- Corner back and end must cut the runner back inside, towards the box.

- Both defensive ends pursue to the depth of the deepest running back.

- Linebacker has to come over and fill the gap between the corner and end, if the back gets outside the end.

- Backside end has to trail the deepest running back, constantly on the lookout for the reverse.

20 Defensive Team Pursuit

Desired Development: reaction to the play; either rush and pass protect, or pursue the run.

Steps:

1. Set-up an offensive unit and a defensive unit.
2. On the snap count, QB either drops back five to seven steps, or tosses for the sweep action to either side.
3. On the drop back, the linemen use pass rush techniques, or rip, swim, or spin, and all backers retreat to the zones of coverage.
4. On the toss sweep all defenders rush, using angles of pursuit.

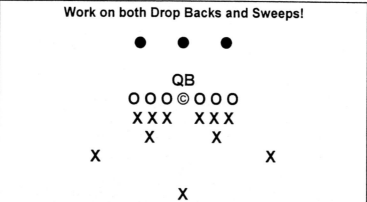

Your Play Name: _____

Key Blocking Assignments

Your Play Name:

Key Blocking Assignments

Introduction

Welcome to the offensive playbook. Following are guidelines for understanding the formats:

- Each play is illustrated on the front and back of each page in different formats. The front side is illustrated in a traditional manner, with symbols as shown below, in the legend. Although it is not literally illustrated in X's and O's, the symbols represent a format commonly used by coaches. The backside of the same play is illustrated with graphic representations of players, a technique which you may find helpful in teaching, especially for the younger kids as explained in Chapter 6. You will notice there is a blank space at the top of this page, which provides you an opportunity to simplify the naming of the play, also explained in Chapter 6, your choice!

- The plays are illustrated with four offensive formations, which I believe are adequate for teaching youth fundamentals: Straight T, Wing T, Pro and Slant I, and the Power I.

- The plays are illustrated against two of the most commonly used youth defensive formations: "6-2 Tight" and "5-2 Okie (Oklahoma)." Obviously, these are just two of the numerous formations your team may face, and blocking assignments may require adjustments against other formations. Refer to the linemen blocking rules in Chapter 4 to help make those adjustments.

- I recommend using one of the formations as your basic offense, and then supplementing those plays with an addition from another formation. For example, if you elect to use the Straight T series, you might also include the 44 Counter Trap and the 34 Wham, both from the Wing T series. Remember, keep it simple!

X	Center	1	QB	DE	Defensive End
G	Offensive Guard	2	Left Halfback Tailback	LB	Linebacker
T	Offensive Tackle	3	Fullback	CB	Cornerback
E	Tight End	4	Right Halfback Wingback, Slotback, Flanker	S	Safety
SE	Split End	DG	Defensive Guard	FS	Free Safety
⌇	Motion	DT	Defensive Tackle	SS	Strong Safety

T - 30 Blast vs 6 - 2 Tight Defense

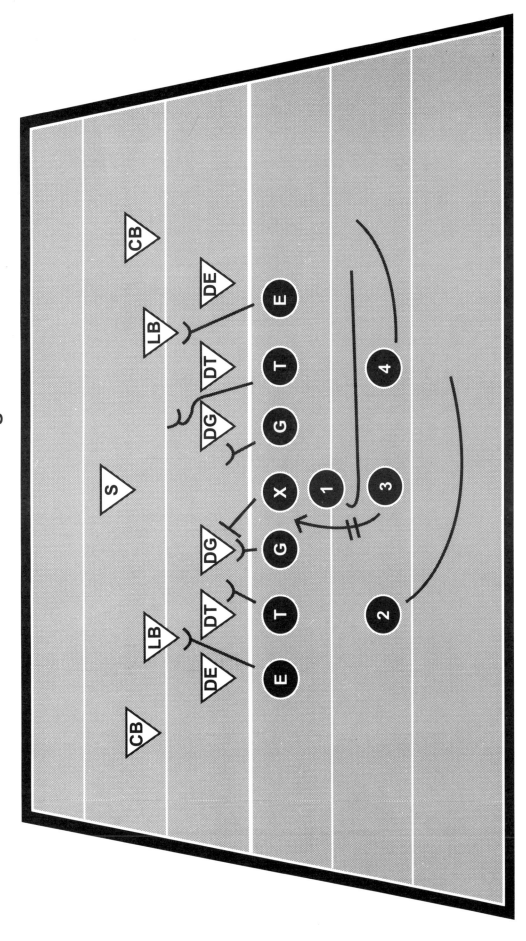

Key Blocking Assignments

- Center and Playside Guard double team the Defensive Tackle out towards the left sideline.
- Playside Tackle blocks Defensive tackle out.
- Playside End crosses neutral zone and attempts to get the Playside Linebacker.
- Backside Guard seals the A gap.
- Backside Tackle and Tight End cross neutral zone and attempt to shield the Linebacker and / or other secondary defenders.
- QB reverse pivots counter clockwise keeping his back to the defense, hands off to Fullback and fakes a toss sweep action with the arm movements to the Left Halfback, trailing him until whistle blows.

T - 30 Blast vs 6 - 2 Tight Defense

T - 44 Quick vs 5 - 2 Okie Defense

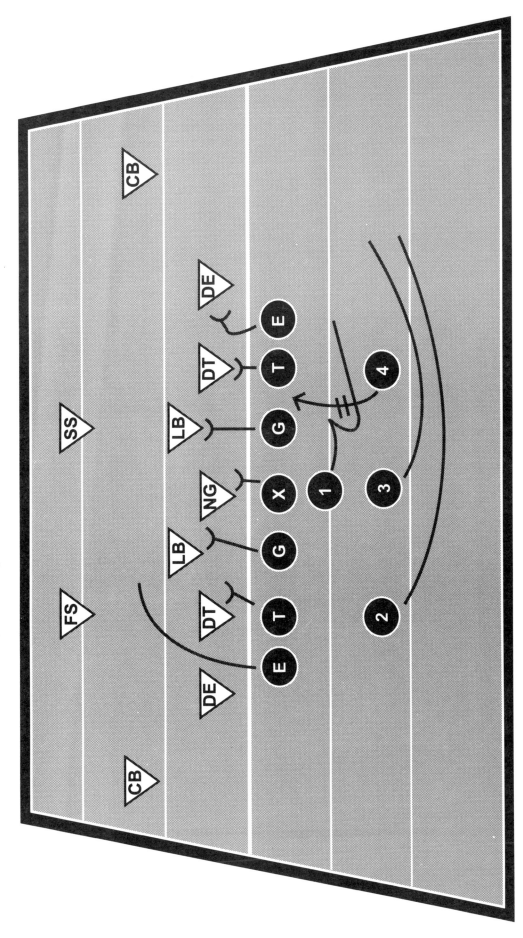

Key Blocking Assignments

- Center steps with the right foot into the A gap and seals off the Noseguard.
- Playside Guard and Tackle drive block straight ahead.
- Playside End kicks out the Defensive End toward the right sideline.
- Backside Guard attempts to shoot to the inside of the Linebacker.
- Backside Tackle and Tight End cross the neutral zone and run toward the right flag to provide shields against the secondary defenders.

- QB opens to 3 o'clock, hands off the Right Halfback, steps 5 o'clock and fakes the sweep action to the right with hands on the outside hip as if he has the ball.
- Left Halfback and Fullback fake the sweep action to the right - Left Halfback positions his hands up as if to receive the toss.

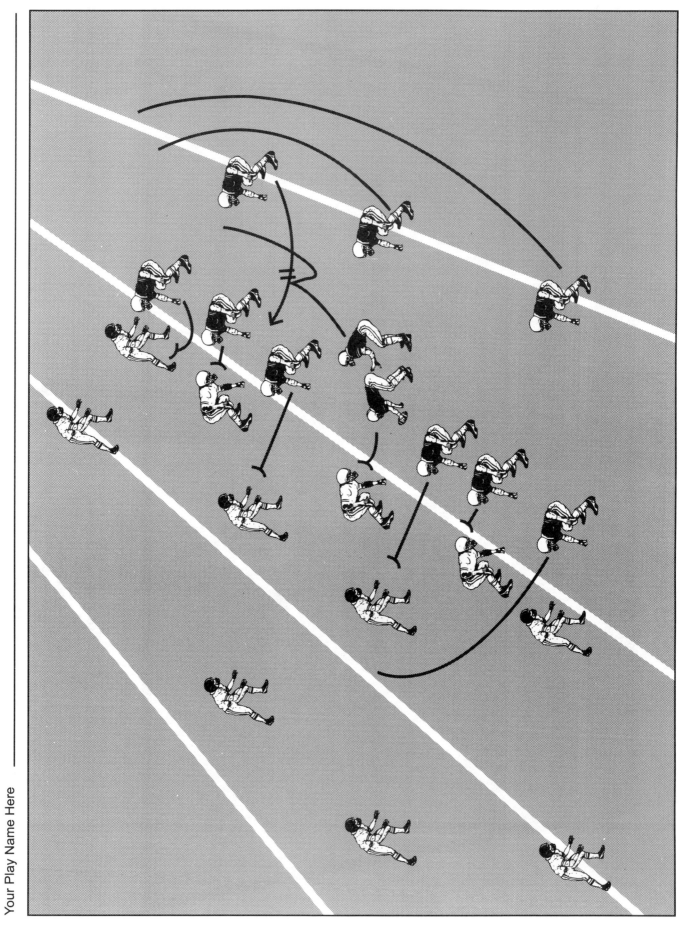

T - 44 Quick vs 5 - 2 Okie Defense

T - 26 Power vs 6 - 2 Tight Defense

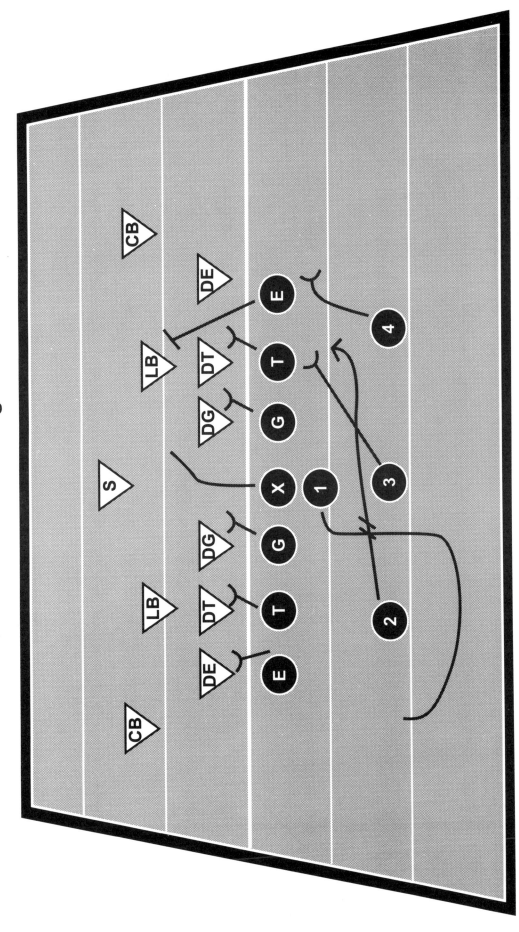

Key Blocking Assignments

- Center and Playside Guard and Tackle seal their outside. If there is no defender in the A gap, the Center should release to the middle of the secondary.
- Playside End slants inside and blocks the inside Linebacker.
- Backside Guard, Tackle and End seal to their inside and release to the middle of the defensive secondary.
- QB opens left to 6 o'clock, hands off to the Left Halfback and fakes a bootleg action left.

- Left Halfback opens with right foot to 2 o'clock, takes the handoff and follows the Fullbacks jersey numbers up through the 6 hole.
- Right Halfback steps with right foot to 2 o'clock and kicks the defensive end out.
- Fullback open steps with the right foot to 2 o'clock and leads up through the 6 hole.

T - 26 Power vs 6 - 2 Tight Defense

T - 28 Sweep vs Okie Defense

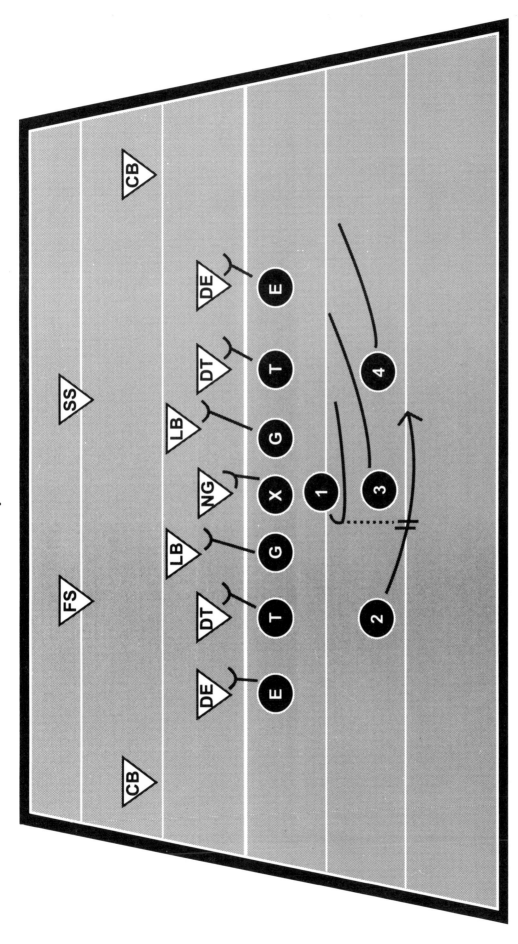

Key Blocking Assignments

- Center steps with the right foot into the A gap and seals off the Noseguard.
- Playside Guard shoots for the outside hip of the inside Linebacker.
- Playside steps to 2 o'clock and hooks the defensive end to the inside.
  Backside Guard and Tight End shoots for the inside hip of the backside linebacker.
- Backside End and Tackle seal to the inside and release to the middle of the defensive secondary.
- QB opens left to 6 o'clock and tosses to left halfback, continues a reverse move towards playside and looks to block first defender across the line of scrimmage.

- Left Halfback opens with right foot to 3 o'clock and receives the toss. As he crosses the line of scrimmage he should look for the chance to cutback towards the middle of the field.

- Right Halfback and Fullback lead the sweep to the right.
  OPTIONAL - 1 or both guards can pull and lead the play against this defense.

T - 28 Sweep vs Okie Defense

T - 43 Trap vs 6 - 2 Tight

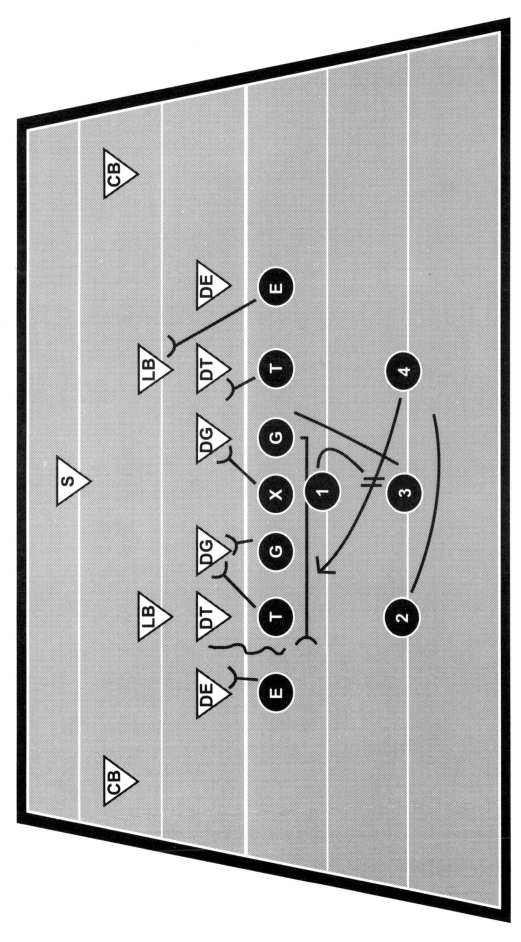

Key Blocking Assignments

- Center steps with right foot to slow the backside Defensive Guard until the Fullback can seal the hole.

- Playside Guard and Tackle double team the Defensive Guard and drive him to the inside. The playside Defensive Tackle is allowed to penetrate into the backfield.

- The Backside Guard pulls left and kicks out the Defensive Tackle.

- The Playside Tight End hits the Defensive End and releases across the neutral zone looking for the Inside Linebacker or Cornerback.

- Backside Tackle seals to the inside and releases to the middle of the secondary.

- QB opens right to 6 o'clock deep enough to allow the Backside Guard to pull down the line, fakes a handoff to the Fullback (keep the back to the defense), and hands off to the Right Halfback, and fakes a bootleg action right.

- Fullback steps to 1 o'clock and fakes a hand off up through the 2 hole and blocks the backside Defensive Guard.

- Right Halfback stays down and takes a jab step to 1 o'clock, hesitates for 1/2 second, executes a right foot crossover step to 10 o'clock and takes the hand off running up through the 3 hole.

- Left Halfback open steps with right foot to 3 o'clock, fakes toss sweep right with the arms and hands up as if to receive the toss.

Your Play Name Here

T - 43 Trap vs 6 - 2 Tight

T - 45 Rollout Pass

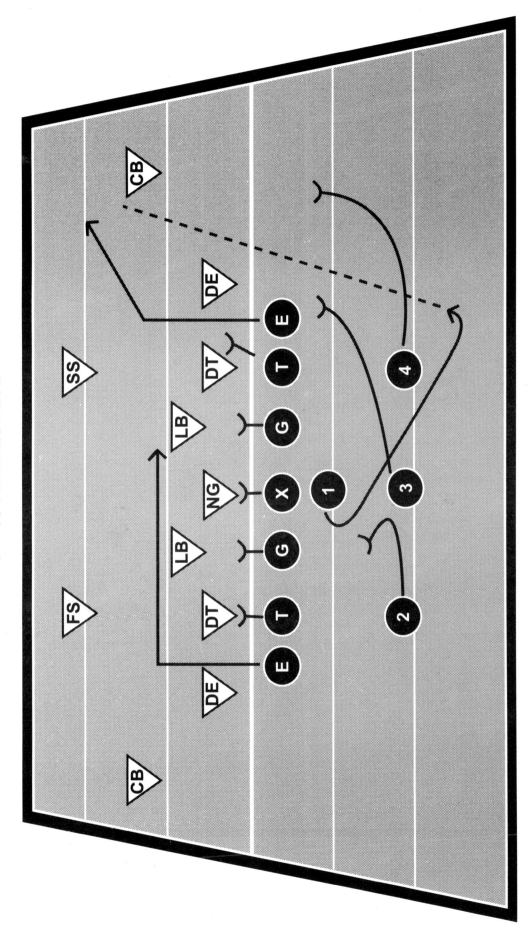

Key Blocking Assignments

- Offensive line - Tackle to Tackle - execute play action pass blocking.
- QB opens with right foot to 6 o'clock and rolls out 6-8 yards deep setting up behind the Offensive End. QB looks first to the Right Tight End on a 5 (flag) route, if not open to the Left Tight End on a 4 (square-in route).
  Remember - these passing plays are numbered left to right for the receivers!

- The Fullback and Right Halfback open to 3 o'clock, move right and provide a blocking wall to protect the QB.
- The Left Halfback opens to 3 o'clock and guards the backside against penetrating defenders.

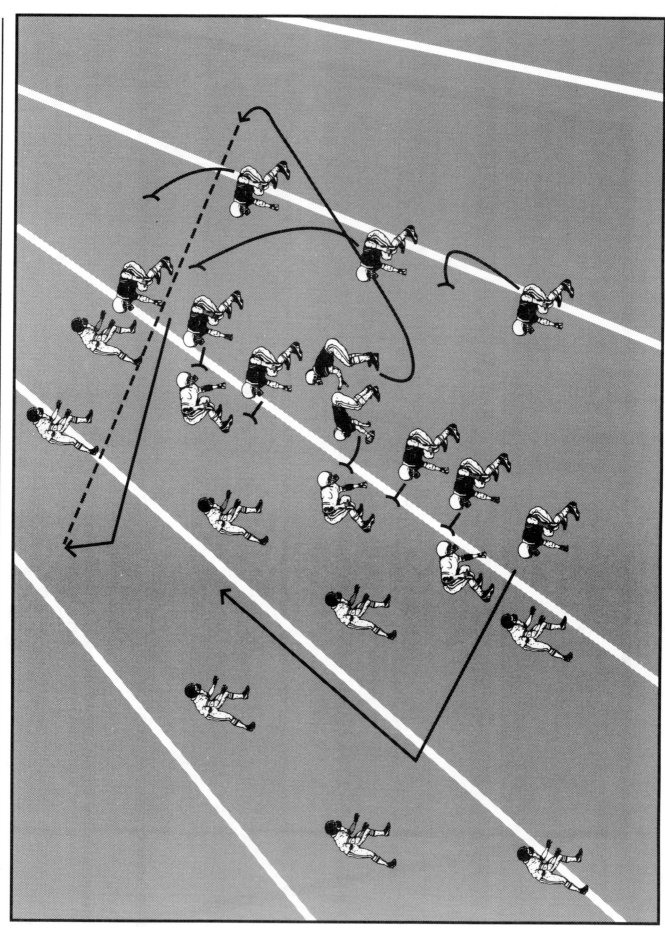

T - 45 Rollout Pass

T - 54 Bootleg Pass

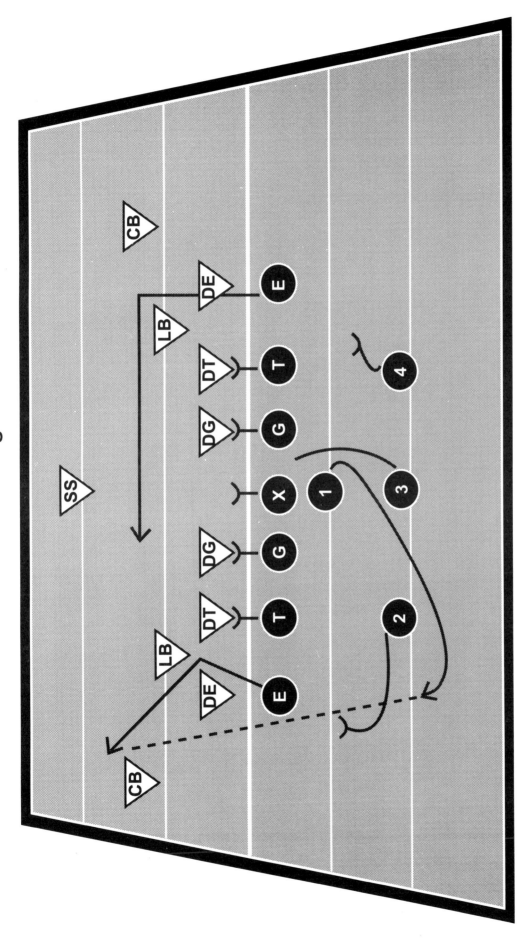

Key Blocking Assignments

- Offensive line - Tackle to Tackle - execute play action pass blocking. QB opens with right foot to 6 o'clock and fakes a handoff to the Fullback through the 2 hole, runs a bootleg action to the left and sets up 6-8 yards deep behind the Left Offensive Tackle. QB looks first to the Left Tight End on a 5 (flag) route, if not to the Right Tight End on a 4 (square-in-route). The Fullback runs a fake handoff through the 2 hole - "rocking the baby".

- The Left Halfback opens to 9 o'clock with the left foot and looks to hook the Defensive End to the inside.
- The Right Halfback guards the backside for penetrating defenders.

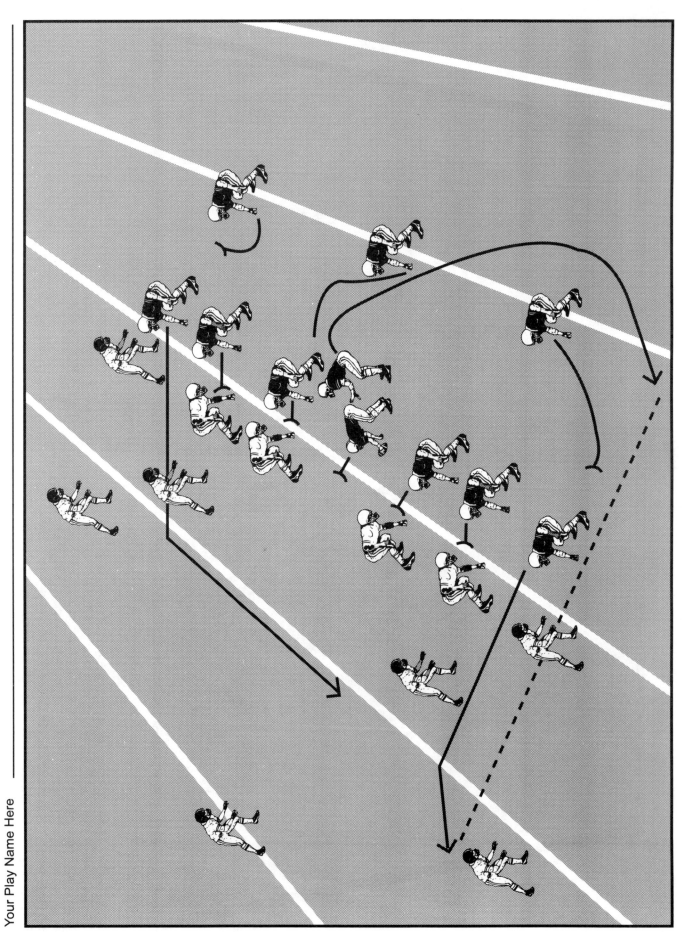

Your Play Name Here

T - 54 Bootleg Pass

Wing T - 24 Trap

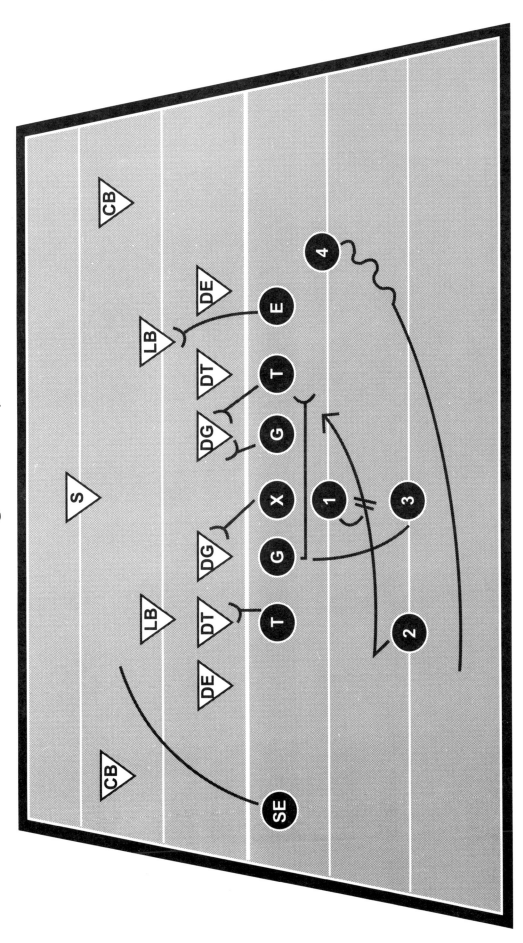

Key Blocking Assignments

- Playside Guard (posts) and Tackle (pivots) double team the Defensive Guard allowing the Defensive Tackle to penetrate.
- Backside Guard pulls left and kicks out the Defensive Tackle.
- Playside Tight End shoots for outside hip of the Inside Linebacker.
- Center seals the left A gap and helps the Diving Fullback stop the Defensive Guard from penetrating.
- Backside Tackle seals the inside gap and releases to the middle of the secondary.

- Backside Split End releases to the middle of the secondary.
- QB opens left to 6 o'clock and fakes a hand off to the Fullback up through the 1 hole, then hands off to the Right Halfback up through the 4 hole.
- Wingback starts in motion after 1 second down count and runs a sweep action left with the arms and hands up as if to receive the toss.
- Left Halfback takes a jab step to the 11 o'clock and cuts back and across the QB taking the hand off and running up through the 4 hole.

Wing T - 24 Trap

Wing T - 45 Buck Sweep

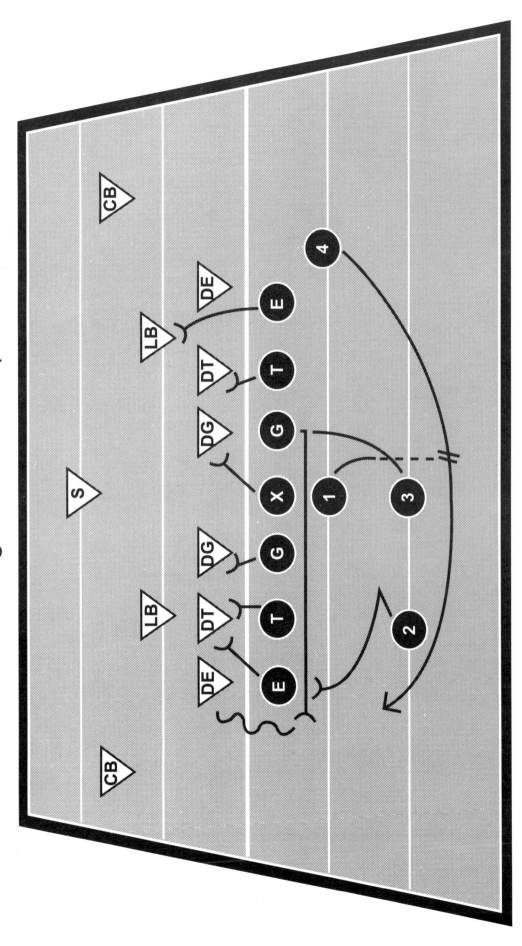

Key Blocking Assignments

- Playside Tight End (pivots) and Tackle (posts) double team the Defensive Tackle allowing the Defensive End to penetrate.
- Backside Guard pulls left and kicks out the Defensive Tackle.
- Playside Guard blocks the Defensive Guard.
- Center seals the right A gap and helps the Diving Fullback stop the Defensive Guard from penetrating.
- Backside Tackle and End seal the inside gap and release to the middle of the secondary.

- QB opens right to 6 o'clock and fakes a hand off to the fullback up through the 2 hole, then tosses to the Wingback in the sweep action.
- Wingback opens with the left foot to 7 o'clock and runs sweep action at a depth of about 6 yards taking the pitch at a point directly behind the Offensive Center.
- Left Halfback takes a jab step to the 2 o'clock and delays for 1 second, then lead blocks for the Wingback up through the 5 hole.

Wing T - 45 Buck Sweep

Wing T - 44 Counter Trap

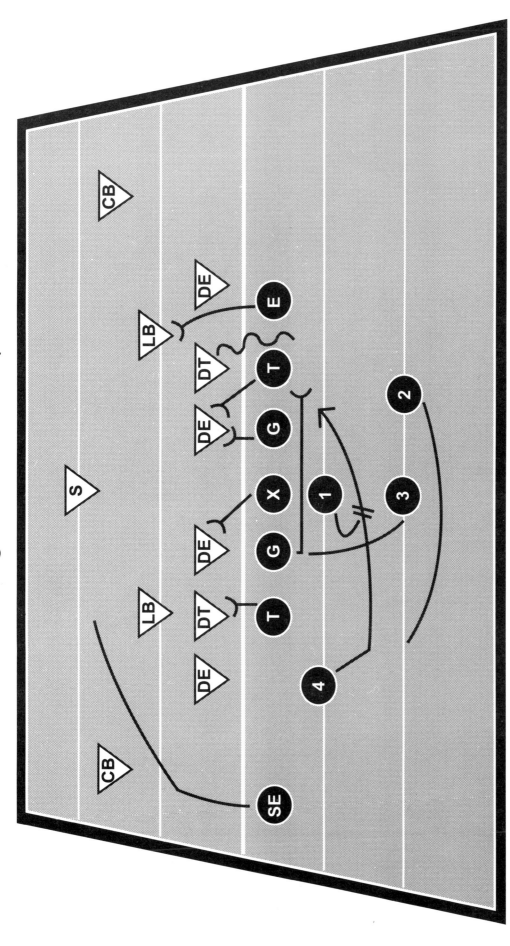

Key Blocking Assignments

- Playside Guard (posts) and Tackle (pivots) double team the Defensive Guard allowing the Defensive Tackle to penetrate.
- Backside Guard pulls left and kicks out the Defensive Tackle.
- Playside Tight End shoots for outside hip of the Inside Linebacker.
- Center seals the left A gap and helps the Diving Fullback stop the Defensive Guard from penetrating.
- Backside Tackle seals the inside gap and releases to the middle of the secondary.

- Backside Split End releases to the middle of the secondary.
- QB opens left to 6 o'clock and fakes a hand off to the Fullback up through the 1 hole, then hands off to the Wingback up through the 4 hole.
- Wingback steps right to 3 o'clock and cuts across the QB taking the hand off and cutting back up into the 4 hole.
- Left Halfback delays momentarily and opens left running a sweep action with the arms and hands up as if to receive the toss.

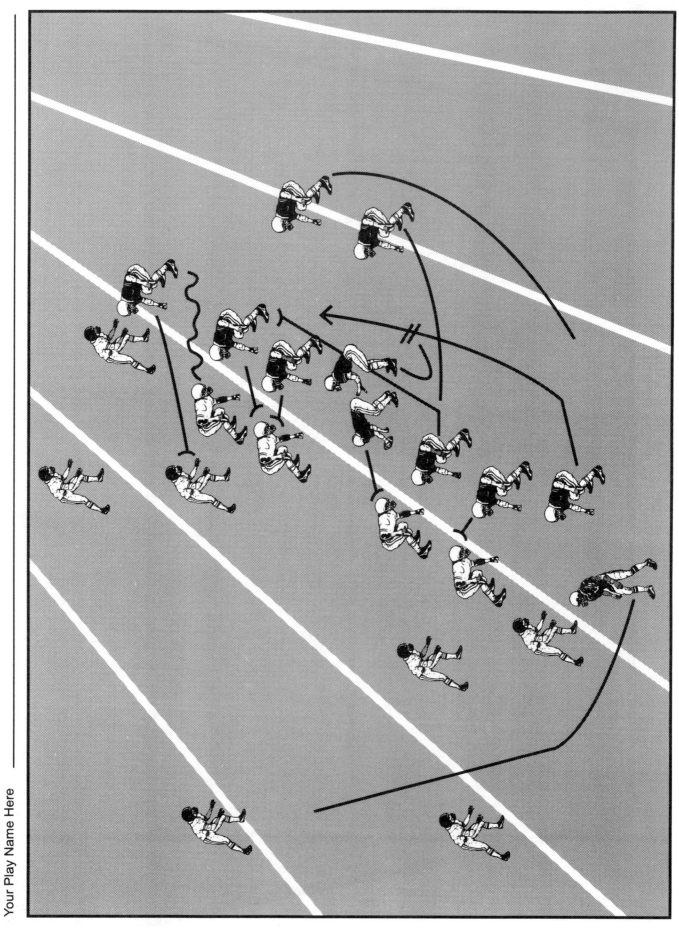

Wing T - 44 Counter Trap

Wing T - 34 Wham vs 6 - 2 Tight Defense

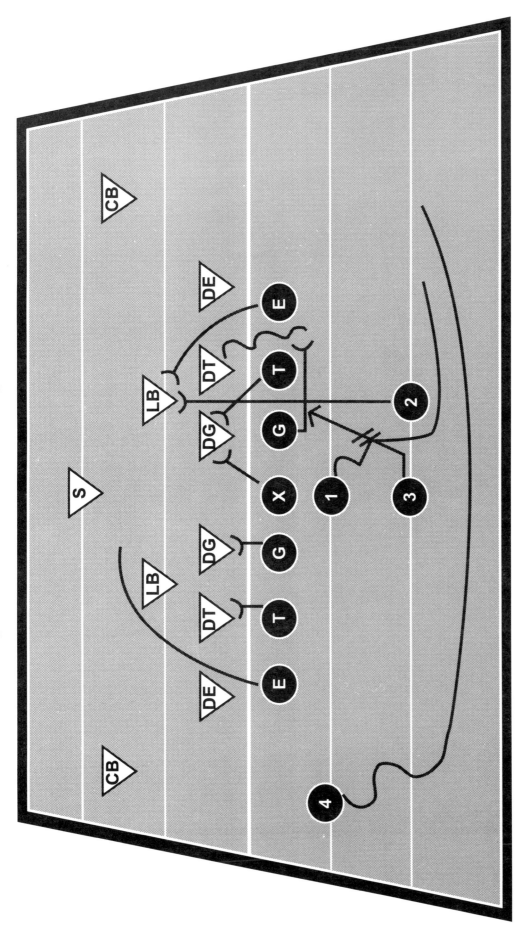

Key Blocking Assignments

- Center and Playside Tackle wedge the Defensive Guard.
- Playside Guard crosses behind Playside Tackle and kicks out Defensive Tackle.
- Playside Tight End shoots for outside shoulder of the Inside Linebacker.
- Backside Linemen seal the inside gap and release to the middle of the secondary.
- QB opens right to 4 o'clock and hands off to the fullback, up through the 4 hole, then runs a sweep action to the right faking a pitch to trailing Wingback.

- Right Halfback runs straight ahead and lead blocks up through the 4 hole.
- Fullback opens right to 3 o'clock, takes 2 steps and cuts back up behind the Right Halfback's trail, takes hand off and runs up through the 4 hole.
- Wingback starts in motion after a 1 second down count and runs a sweep action right with the arms and hands up as if to receive the toss.

Wing T - 34 Wham vs 6 - 2 Tight Defense

Wing T - 345 Throwback vs 5 - 2 Oklahoma Defense

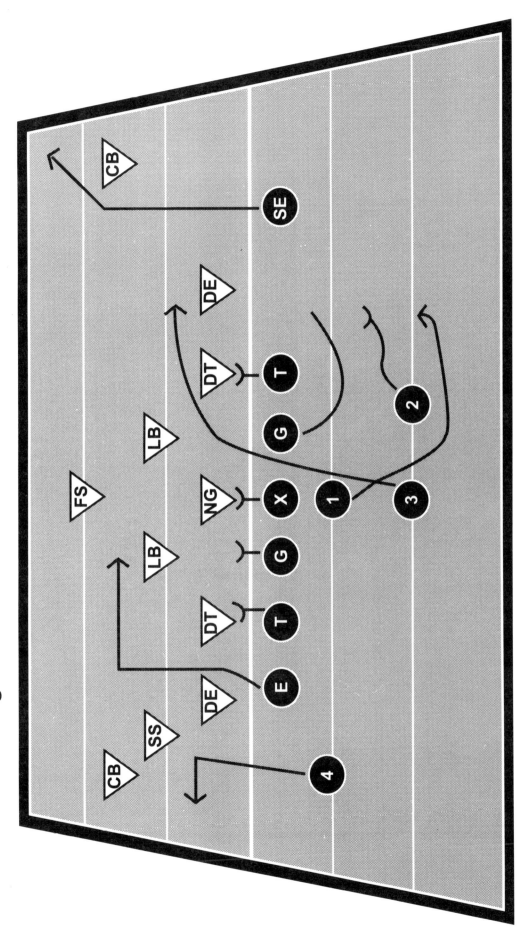

Key Blocking Assignments

- Playside Guard pulls right and to the outside to help pass protect.
- Tackle - Tackle executes drop back pass protection techniques.
- Wingback runs a 3 (square out) route.
- Left Tight End runs a 4 (square in) route.
- Right Split End runs a 5 (flag) route.
- Fullback takes a fake hand off through 2 hole and runs across the neutral zone cutting outside underneath the Linebacker and to the flat.

- QB opens right to 5 o'clock and fakes a hand off to the Fullback up through the 2 hole, then rolls out to a 7 step depth and sets up to throw. Looks for receivers in the following order: Split End first, Fullback in the flat second.
- Right Halfback swings right to provide pass protection.

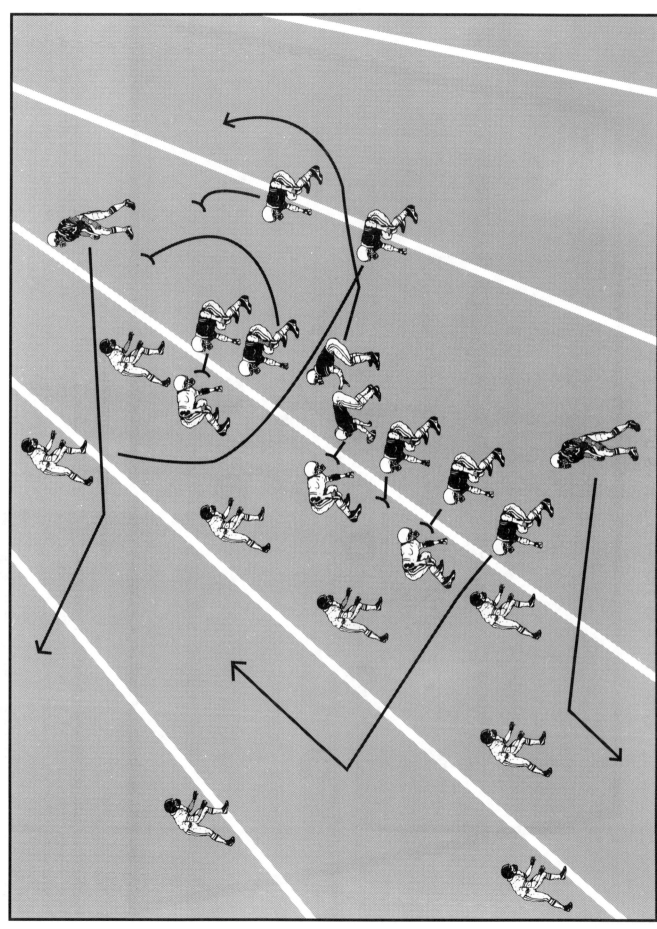

Wing - T 345 Throwback vs 5 - 2 Oklahoma Defense

Pro I - 26 Power vs 5 - 2 Okie Defense

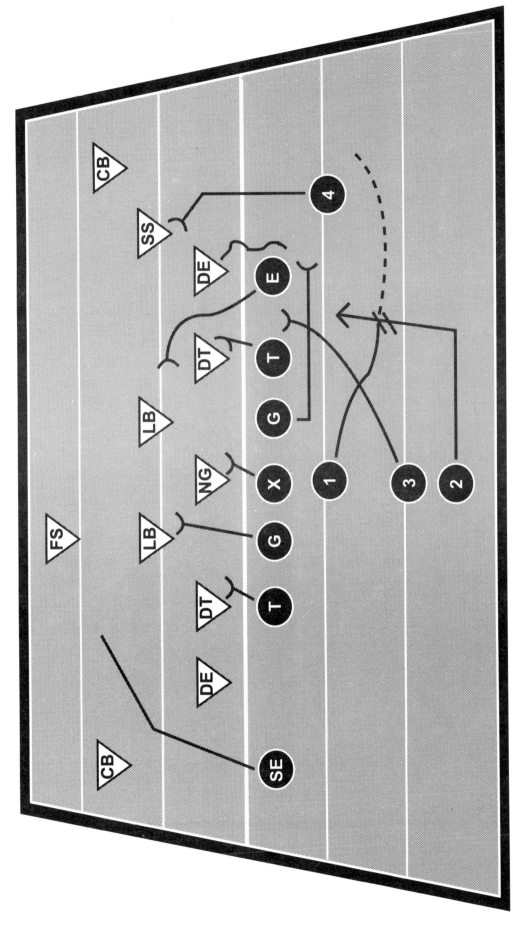

Key Blocking Assignments

- Center seals the A gap against the Noseguard.
- Playside Guard pulls right and kicks out the defensive end.
- Playside Tackle seals the C gap against the Defensive Tackle.
- Playside Tight End shoots for the outside hip of the Inside Linebacker.
- Backside Guard shoots for the inside hip of the Linebacker.
- Backside Tackle seals the B gap and releases to the middle of the secondary.

- Backside Split End releases into the seam between the Cornerback and Safety.
- Flanker runs at the Strong Safety and hits on his inside shoulder.
- Fullback steps to 2 o'clock and leads up through the 6 hole.
- QB open steps right to 4 o'clock, runs deep and hands off to the Tailback through the 6 hole, and continues with sweep action.
- Tailback opens with the right foot to 3 o'clock, runs 3-4 steps laterally and uses a crossover to cut up through the 6 hole.

Pro I - 26 Power vs 5 - 2 Okie Defense

Slot I - 31 Blast vs 6 - 2 Tight Defense

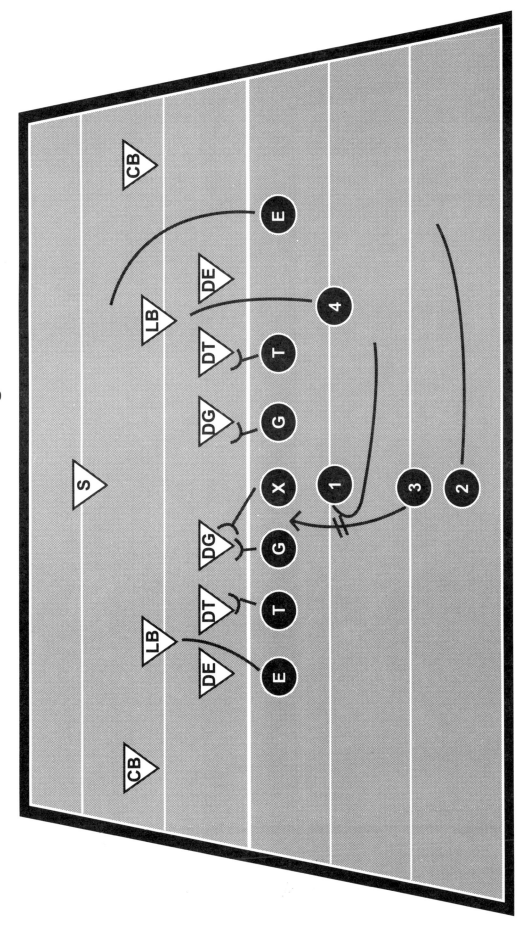

Key Blocking Assignments

- Playside Guard (posts) and Center (pivot) double team the Defensive Guard.
- Playside Tackle seals the B gap against the Defensive Tackle.
- Playside Tight End shoots for the inside hip of the Inside Linebacker.
- Backside Guard shoots seals the A gap against the Defensive Guard.
- Backside Tackle seals the B gap and releases to the middle of the secondary.
- Backside Slotback runs at the Inside Linebacker.

- Backside Split End releases into the seam between the Cornerback and Safety.
- QB reverse pivots counter clockwise hands off to the Fullback through the 1 hole, and continues with a toss sweep action to the right.
- Fullback steps to 11 o'clock, takes the hand off and runs up through the 1 hole.
- Tailback opens with the right foot to 3 o'clock, fakes toss sweep right with the arms and hands up as if to receive the toss.

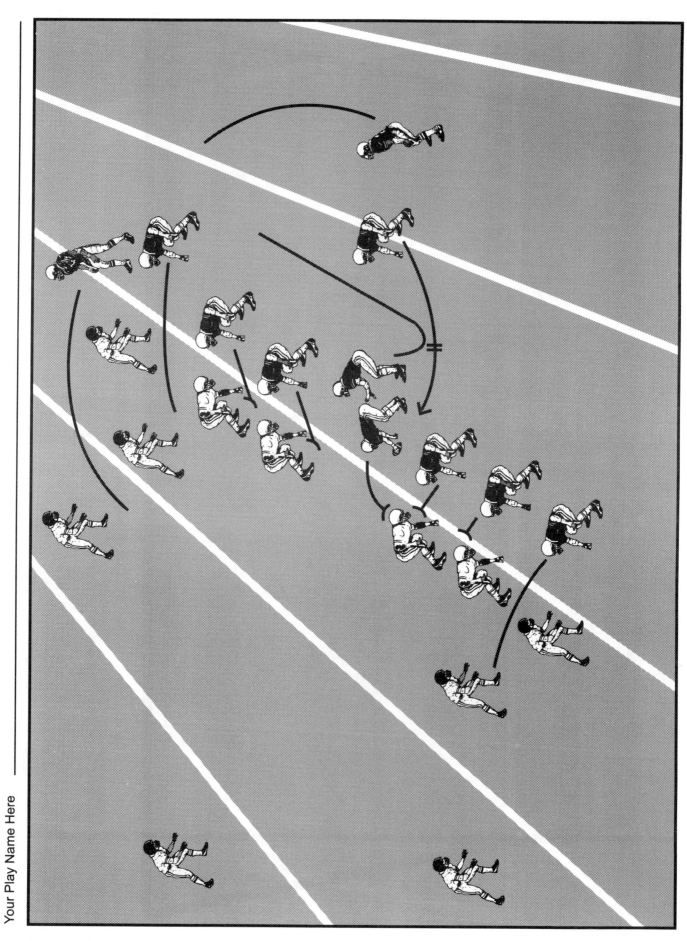

Slot I - 31 Blast vs 6 Tight Defense

Pro I - 28 Toss Sweep vs 6 - 2 Tight Defense

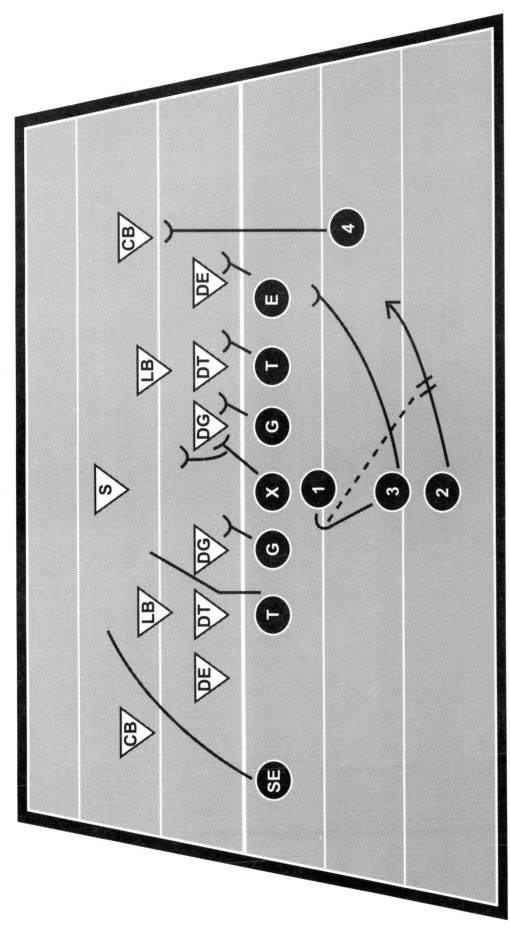

Key Blocking Assignments

- Center and Playside Guard and Tackle seal their outside gap. If no defender in the A gap, Center releases to the middle of the secondary.
- Playside Right End attempts to hook the Defensive End to the inside.
- Backside Guard and Tackle seal to the inside and release to the middle of the secondary.
- Backside Split End releases into the seam between the Cornerback and Safety.
- Flanker runs at the Cornerback.

- Fullback leads the sweep to the outside taking the first defender across the line of scrimmage into the backfield.
- QB reverse pivots counter clockwise and tosses to the Tailback, and follows the pitch in case it is fumbled.
- Tailback opens with the right foot to 3 o'clock and receives the toss. As he crosses the line of scrimmage he should look for the chance to cutback towards the middle of the field.

Pro I - 28 Toss Sweep vs 6 - 2 Tight Defense

Slot I - 43 Counter vs Okie Defense

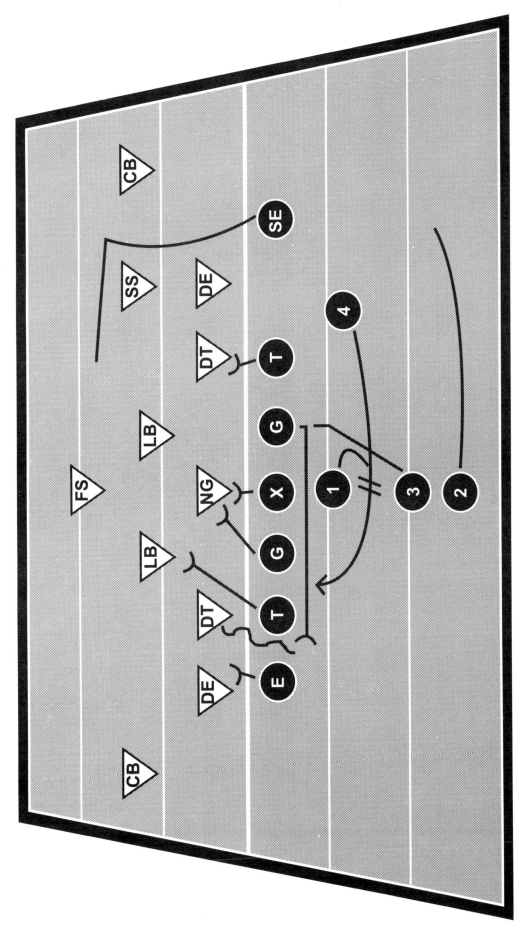

Key Blocking Assignments

- Center (posts) and Playside Guard (pivot) double team the Noseguard. Playside Tackle attacks the Inside Linebacker allowing the Defensive Tackle to penetrate.
- Playside Tight End kicks out the Defensive End and releases toward the Cornerback.
- Backside Guard pulls left and kicks out (traps) the penetrating Defensive Tackle.
- Backside Tackle seals the B gap and releases to the middle of the secondary.

- Backside Split End runs the seam in between the Strong Safety and Cornerback.
- QB opens right to 4 o'clock, fakes a hand off to the Fullback up through the 2 hole, and hands off to the Slotback.
- Slotback opens left to 9 o'clock and runs across the QB taking the hand off and cutting up into the 3 hole.
- Tailback opens with the right foot to 3 o'clock fakes toss sweep right with the arms and hands up as if to receive the toss.

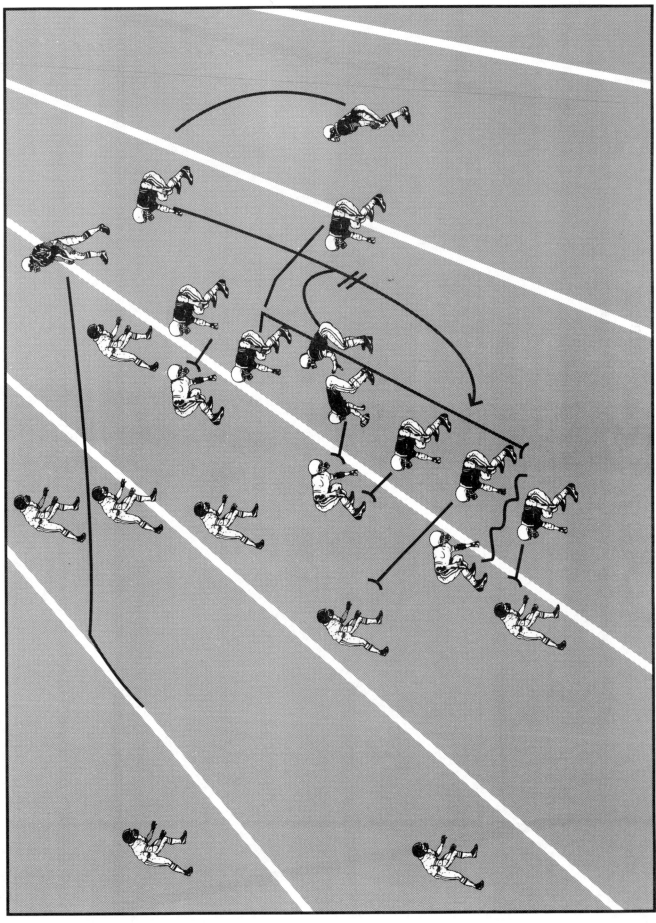

Slot I - 43 Counter vs Okie Defense

Pro I - 436 Drag vs 6 - 2 Tight Defense

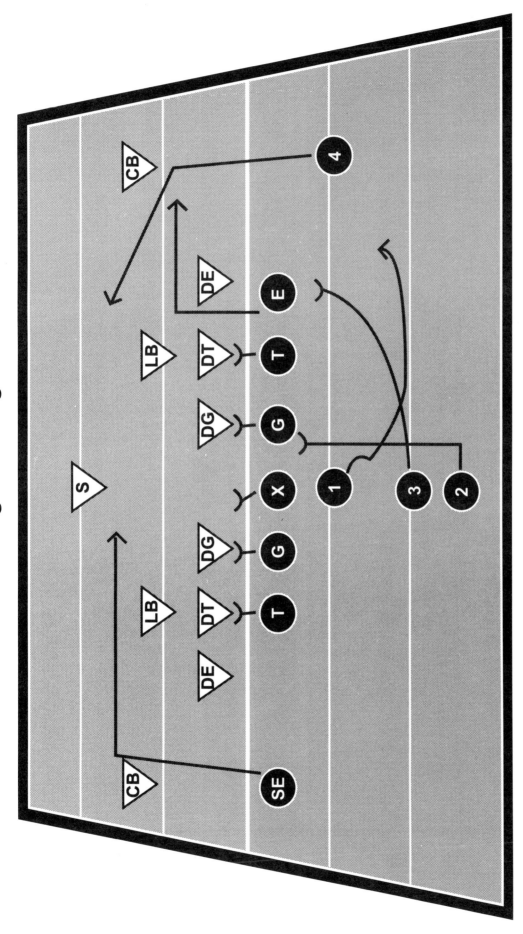

Key Blocking Assignments

- Tackle to Tackle execute drop back pass protection.
- Left Split End runs a 4 (square in) route.
- Right Tight End runs a 3 (square out) route.
- Flanker runs a 6 (post) route.

- Fullback opens right to 3 o'clock and swings out to stop the defensive end's penetration.
- QB opens right to 6 o'clock and fakes a hand off to the Tailback up through the 2 hole, roles out to 7 steps deep and sets up to throw looking to the Receivers in the following order: 3 first, and 4 second.

Pro I - 436 Drag vs 6 - 2 Tight Defense

Pro I - 866 Slant vs 6 - 2 Tight Defense

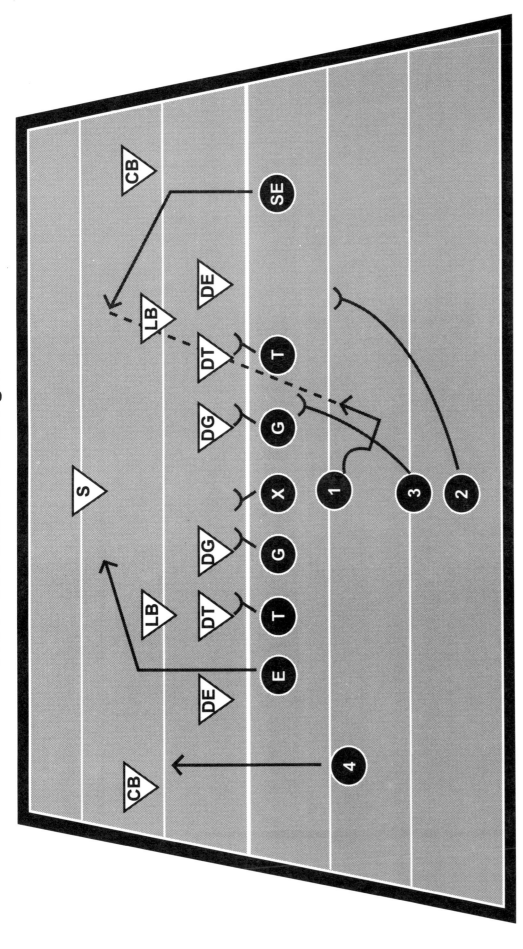

Key Blocking Assignments

- Offensive line - Tackle to Tackle - execute play action pass blocking, staying low and into the thigh area to allow the QB more vision.
- Flanker runs a 8 (fly) route.
- Left Tight End runs a 6 (post) route.
- Right Split End runs a 6 (post / slant-in) route getting in the seam behind the Linebacker and between the Safety and Cornerback.
- Fullback takes a fake hand off into the 4 hole, also staying low. Tailback opens to a 4 o'clock and runs at the Defensive End.
- QB opens with the right foot to 3 o'clock, fakes the hand off to the Fullback, drops 3 steps and hits the Split End on the Post / Slant route.

Pro I - 866 Slant vs 6 - 2 Tight Defense

Power I - 25 Cutback vs 6 - 2 Tight Defense

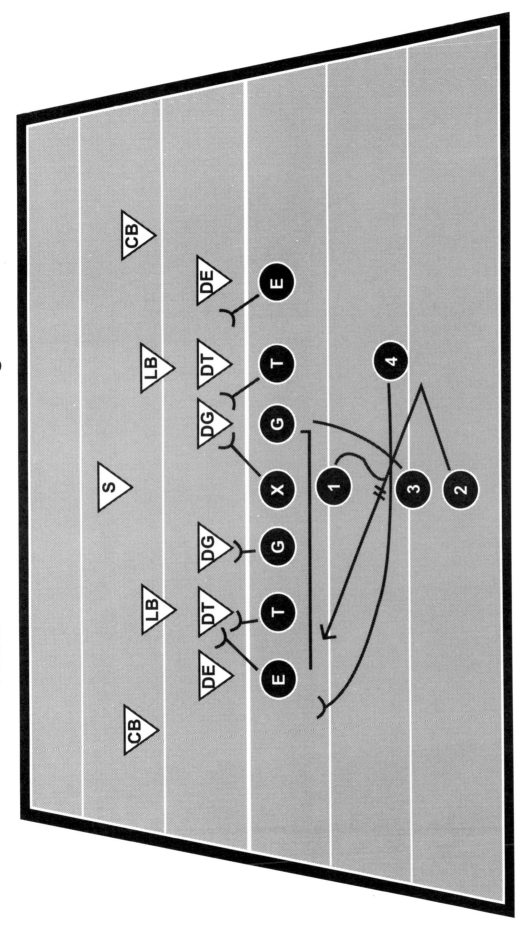

Key Blocking Assignments

- Playside Guard blocks Defensive Guard.
- Playside Tackle (posts) and Tight End (pivots) the Defensive tackle allowing the Defensive End to penetrate.
- Backside Guard pulls left and kicks out (traps) the penetrating Defensive End.
- Backside Tackle and Tight End seal the inside gaps and release to the middle of the secondary.
- QB opens right to 4 o'clock, fakes a hand off to the Fullback up through the 2 hole, and hands off to the Tailback.

- Right Halfback jab steps to 2 o'clock with the right foot then uses crossover step to 9 o'clock and runs across the QB lead blocking for the Tailback up into the 5 hole.
- Tailback opens with the right foot to 2 o'clock, takes 1-2 more steps and uses a crossover step to cutback into a path trailing the right halfback, takes the hand off left and up through the 5 hole.

Your Play Name Here

Power I - 25 Cutback vs 6 - 2 Tight Defense

Power I - 18 Sweep 5 - 2 Oklahoma Defense

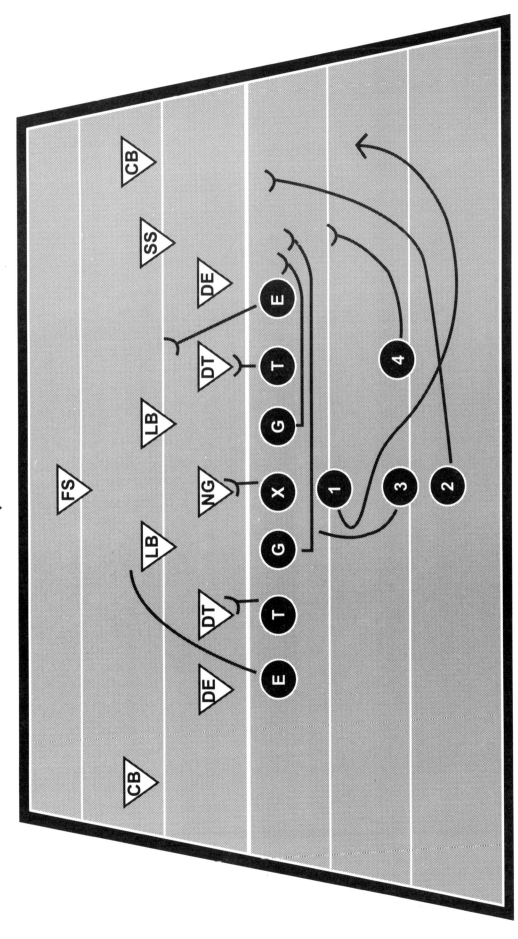

Key Blocking Assignments

- Playside and Backside Guards pull right looking for first defender penetrating into the backfield.
- Playside Tackle blocks on the Defensive Tackle sealing the outside gap.
- Playside Tight End shoots for the Inside Linebacker's outside hip.
- Backside Tackle and End seal the inside gap and release to the middle of the secondary.

- QB reverse pivots counter clockwise, fakes a hand off to the full back up through the 1 hole and sweeps right at a depth of 4-6 yards from the line of scrimmage.
- Right Halfback steps to 3 o'clock with the right foot moves toward the line of scrimmage looking for the penetration of the Defensive End or Strong Safety.
- Tailback opens with the right foot to 3 o'clock and trails off the outside hip of the right Halfback to lead block for the QB.

Power I - 18 Sweep vs 5 - 2 Oklahoma Defense

Power I 26 Cross Buck

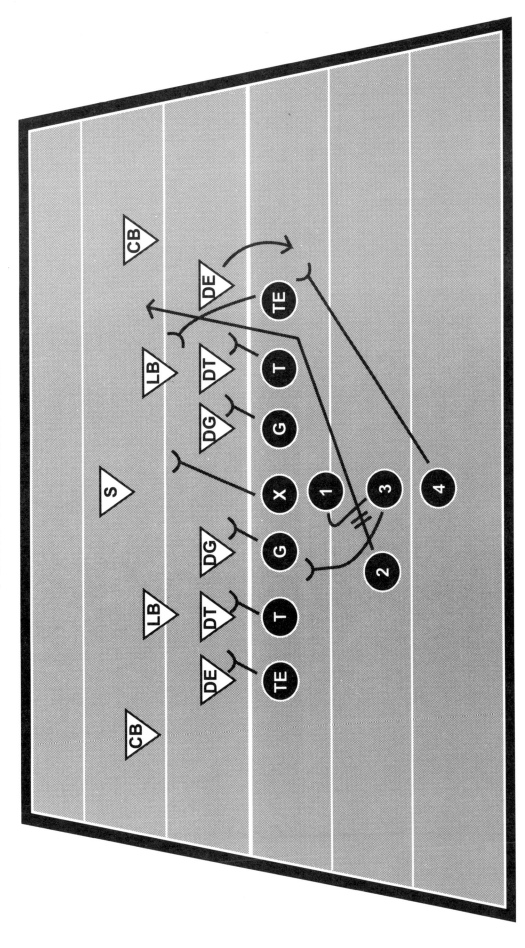

Key Blocking Assignments

- Center, Playside Guard and Tackle seal the outside gap.
- Playside Tight End shoots for the outside hip of the inside Linebacker.
- Backside Guard, Tackle, and End seal the inside gap and release to the middle of the secondary.
- Tailback opens with the right foot to 2 o'clock and kicks out the Defensive End.

- QB reverse pivots counter clockwise, fakes a hand off to the Fullback up through the 1 hole, and hands off to the Left Halfback.
- Left Halfback jab steps with the left foot to 11 o'clock, then uses a crossover step to 2 o'clock and runs across the QB taking the hand off up through the 6 hole.

Your Play Name Here

Power I - 26 Cross Buck

Power I - 46 Dropback vs 5 - 2 Okie Defense

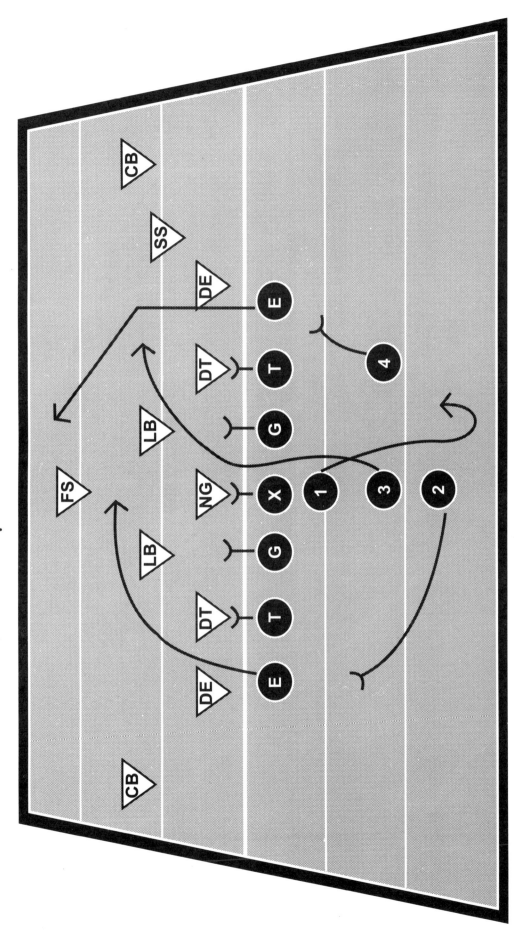

Key Blocking Assignments

- QB opens right to 6 o'clock and fakes a hand off to the Fullback who runs up through the 2 hole and out to the flat. QB drops back 7 steps and sets to throw looking to the open Receivers in the following order: 6 first, 4 second Fullback to Flat last.
  - Right Halfback sets up pass protection to the right.
  - Tailback sets up pass protection to the left.

- Tackle to Tackle execute dropback pass protection.
- Left Tight End runs a 4 (square in) route.
- Right Tight End runs a 6 (post) route.

Power I - 46 Dropback vs 5 - 2 Okie Defense

APPENDIX

Key Game Rules And Penalty Summary

Summary	Loss of Yards
1. **FAILURE TO PROPERLY WEAR REQUIRED EQUIPMENT** - The most common violation is failure to keep a mouth piece in the mouth prior to or during the snap.	5
2. **DELAY OF GAME** - Action, or inaction, which delays putting the ball in play. The most common cause is failing to snap the ball within 25 seconds after the umpire signals the ball is ready for play.	5
3. **ENCROACHMENT** - This can be charged against the offense or defense. When the ball is ready for play, no player, except the offensive center, may have any part of his body crossing the plane of the neutral zone. Players occasionally line up in the neutral zone, which results in a penalty.	5
4. **FALSE START** - This occurs when an offensive player moves prior to the snap, except a legal motion by a running back. The rule is intended to prevent the offense from simulating a movement which will cause the defender to encroach into the neutral zone. A common example is when a down offensive lineman moves his hand, or shifts after he has been down and set.	5
5. **LESS THAN SEVEN OFFENSIVE PLAYERS ON THE LINE OF SCRIMMAGE** - The offense is required to have exactly seven players aligned on the line of scrimmage at the snap of the ball. Occasionally, a player will line up too deep into the backfield resulting in less than the seven required players.	5
6. **ILLEGAL MOTION** - Only one offensive running back may be in motion at the time the ball is snapped. In addition, he must be moving laterally and have been set for one full second before beginning the motion.	5
7. **ILLEGAL USE OF THE HANDS** - There are many uses which are prohibited. One example is that neither offensive nor defensive players, except for the offensive running back, may strike an opponent's helmet with his hands.	5
8. **HOLDING** - Neither offensive nor defensive players may use his hands to grasp an opponent in an attempt to restrain him.	10
9. **UNSPORTSMANLIKE CONDUCT** - The types of actions which can incur this penalty include, but are not limited to, using profanity, taunting an opponent, intentionally kicking at the ball, refusing to comply with an official.	10
10. **CLIPPING** - This is charging or falling into the backside of the opponent, unless he is a running back. The only exception is if it occurs in the "Free Blocking Zone," which is an area that is rectangular and extends laterally four yards to either side of the spot of the snap, and three yards behind each line of scrimmage.	15
11. **FACE TACKLE OR SPEAR** - Players are not allowed to use the helmet to intentionally use the helmet to face tackle, spear, butt or ram the opponent.	15
12. **FIGHTING** - No player is allowed to fight.	15 Expulsion

Player Evaluation

FUN	• Really enjoys playing the game • Seems to really enjoy being at practice
ATTITUDE	• Strong desire to play and compete - has the confidence to face off with opposition • Does what coaches ask him to do without hesitation
SKILLS	**STRENGTHS** • Good execution of stance and footwork • Is continuing to improve his blocking with quickness and contact • Excellent offensive & defensive guard • Has learned and progressed since season began • Exceptional confidence in his ability to compete against anyone **DEVELOPMENT AREAS** • Work on understanding the role of the positions he plays and how important it is to team success • Stay low on blocks and put defender on the ground • On defense work on shedding the opponent and getting into the backfield - I want to see him make more tackles • Ask questions when in doubt - open up more to the coaches and say what's on his mind • Realize his talents for aggressiveness & hitting and put them to use
TEAMWORK	• Well respected by teammates • Is looked upon as one who can be counted on to make the play
OVERALL	• Super young man and a pleasure to coach - we're really proud of him! • Has a great future in youth sports - I hope he plays other sports as well as football • I've really enjoyed working with him and I and hope he truly is having fun and learning • I predict he will be great if he really enjoys it!

Player Evaluation

Youth Football Safety

Foreword

An injured athlete is every coach's fear. Whether you're working with children, or coaching this country's elite athletes, you feel responsible for making sure your athletes are safe in practice, and in competition.

But sports-related injuries can, and do occur. Your best defense against injury is a good offense; that means being prepared!

American Red Cross

Learning principles of injury prevention and first aid steps for specific emergency situations are an integral part of sport safety. The American Red Cross and the United States Olympic Committee, through a combined effort, have developed the **SPORT SAFETY TRAINING.** Contact your local American Red Cross for details!

Facts

General causes of sports injuries include:

- Unsafe conditions, such as playing surface, equipment, or weather conditions.

- Unsafe actions by athletes during play, such as unnecessary roughness, breaking the rules, etc.

- A lack of proper supervision.

- Use of improper techniques.

- Returning to play before an injury is healed or rehabilitated properly.

About one half of all sports injuries are PREVENTABLE!

Returning To Play

If an athlete has been injured or ill, but <u>seems</u> to have recovered, the coach should assess whether or not the athlete can safely return to play. Keys for helping to make that assessment include:

- Discourage the athlete from returning to play if there is doubt concerning his ability to participate.

Returning To Play, *continued*

- Know when an injury requires medical attention.

- Remember, the absence of pain does not signify the injury is not serious.

- When an injury causes pain, swelling, or redness, do not ask the athlete to try to "walk it off." Movement may aggravate the condition.

Safety Plan

- Have an action plan which includes:

    - ☑ Encouraging coaches to participate in First Aid & Safety certification training.
    - ☑ Recognizing an emergency situation exists and taking action.
    - ☑ An emergency number that is easily accessible, either 911 or another local number.
    - ☑ Providing appropriate care until qualified medical personnel can respond.

- Always inspect equipment before use.

- Train the athletes on proper equipment use, safety procedures, and risks.

- Have athletes warm up prior to play.

Responding To An Injury

- Know what types of injuries are life threatening and need EMERGENCY CARE: breathing difficulties, cardiac arrest, severe bleeding, heat injuries, head/neck/back injuries.

- Keep the player calm, and try to prevent movement, until the assessment can be made and care provided.

- Never attempt to move the player if there is uncertainty about injury to the head, neck or back.

For Kid's Sake
Teaching Tackle Football
The Youth Coach's Field Manual
ISBN 0-9659985-0-9

Next Day Air &
Second Day Air Available!

Yes, please send me a copy of
For Kid's Sake
Teaching Tackle Football
The Youth Coach's Field Manual

Name _____
Street _____Apt_____
City _____State _____Zip_____

Recommended by
The National Youth Sports
Coaches Association

Mail this card today or share it with a friend for additional copies	For Kid's Sake _____ (No. of copies) @ $23.95 _____ **Shipping and Handling Charges** Add $4.00 for 1st copy and add $1.00 for each additional copy. 5 or more, please call 1-888-444-4345

LA Residents Add
8.25% Sales Tax _____
Shipping _____
Total _____

❑ Check or Money Order Enclosed ❑ Visa ❑ MasterCard
Card #_____Exp_____
Signature_____Phone. _____

VISA and Master Card Orders - By Phone Call 1-888-444-4345 Or By FAX (504) 727-2322
Make Checks Payable To: Youth Sports Press, Inc.
Mail to: Youth Sports Press, Inc. • 3433 Hwy. 190 #285 • Mandeville, LA 70471

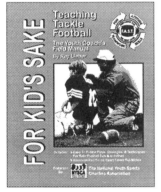

For Kid's Sake
Teaching Tackle Football
The Youth Coach's Field Manual
ISBN 0-9659985-0-9

Next Day Air &
Second Day Air Available!

Yes, please send me a copy of
For Kid's Sake
Teaching Tackle Football
The Youth Coach's Field Manual

Name _____
Street _____Apt_____
City _____State _____Zip_____

Recommended by
The National Youth Sports
Coaches Association

Mail this card today or share it with a friend for additional copies	For Kid's Sake _____ (No. of copies) @ $23.95 _____ **Shipping and Handling Charges** Add $4.00 for 1st copy and add $1.00 for each additional copy. 5 or more, please call 1-888-444-4345

LA Residents Add
8.25% Sales Tax _____
Shipping _____
Total _____

❑ Check or Money Order Enclosed ❑ Visa ❑ MasterCard
Card #_____Exp_____
Signature_____Phone. _____

VISA and Master Card Orders - By Phone Call 1-888-444-4345 Or By FAX (504) 727-2322
Make Checks Payable To: Youth Sports Press, Inc.
Mail to: Youth Sports Press, Inc. • 3433 Hwy. 190 #285 • Mandeville, LA 70471

For Kid's Sake
Teaching Tackle Football
The Youth Coach's Field Manual
ISBN 0-9659985-0-9

Next Day Air &
Second Day Air Available!

Yes, please send me a copy of
For Kid's Sake
Teaching Tackle Football
The Youth Coach's Field Manual

Name _____
Street _____Apt_____
City _____State _____Zip_____

Recommended by
The National Youth Sports
Coaches Association

Mail this card today or share it with a friend for additional copies	For Kid's Sake _____ (No. of copies) @ $23.95 _____ **Shipping and Handling Charges** Add $4.00 for 1st copy and add $1.00 for each additional copy. 5 or more, please call 1-888-444-4345

LA Residents Add
8.25% Sales Tax _____
Shipping _____
Total _____

❑ Check or Money Order Enclosed ❑ Visa ❑ MasterCard
Card #_____Exp_____
Signature_____Phone. _____

VISA and Master Card Orders - By Phone Call 1-888-444-4345 Or By FAX (504) 727-2322
Make Checks Payable To: Youth Sports Press, Inc.
Mail to: Youth Sports Press, Inc. • 3433 Hwy. 190 #285 • Mandeville, LA 70471

PLACE STAMP HERE. POSTAL SERVICE WILL NOT DELIVER WITHOUT POSTAGE

YOUTH SPORTS PRESS, INC.
3733 HWY. 190 # 285
MANDEVILLE, LA 70471

PLACE STAMP HERE. POSTAL SERVICE WILL NOT DELIVER WITHOUT POSTAGE

YOUTH SPORTS PRESS, INC.
3733 HWY. 190 # 285
MANDEVILLE, LA 70471

PLACE STAMP HERE. POSTAL SERVICE WILL NOT DELIVER WITHOUT POSTAGE

YOUTH SPORTS PRESS, INC.
3733 HWY. 190 # 285
MANDEVILLE, LA 70471